Greetings from Lappland

Nils-Aslak Valkeapää

Other Books and Records by Nils-Aslak Valkeapää

Books

Terveisiä Lapista (Otava, Helsinki 1971)
Helsing frå Sameland (Pax forlag, Oslo 1979: translated by Live Hatle)
Gida ijat čuov'gadat (poems) (Oulu 1974: illustrated by author)
Kevään vöt niin valoisat (Helsinki 1980: translated by A. Rosell)
Lávlo vizar biello-cizás (poems) (Sabemelaš-doaimahus, 1976)
Adjaga silbasuohat (poems) illustrated by the author (Vuovjjuš, Karesuando 1980)

Records

1968: *Joikuja* (Otava, Helsinki)
1973: *Jouigamat* (N.-A. Valkeapaa and su juoigan doak'ki)
1975: *Vuoi, Biret-Maret, vuoi*
1976: *De čabba niegut runiidit* (with Asa Blind and Jaakko Gauriloff)
1976: *Duvva-Ailen Niga Elle ja Áillohaš*
1978: *Sami Eatnan duoddariid* (Indigenous Records)
1982: *Sápmi, vuoi Sápmi Aillohažžat* (N.-A. Valkeapää and Áilu A. Gaup)

Greetings from Lappland

The Sami — Europe's Forgotten People

Nils-Aslak Valkeapää

Translated by Beverley Wahl

Zed Press, 57 Caledonian Road, London N1 9DN.

Greetings from Lappland was first published in Finland by Otava, Helsinki, 1971 (new revised edition, 1978) and in Norway by Pax Forlag, Oslo, 1979. First published in English with a New Introduction and photographs by Zed Press, 57 Caledonian Road, London N1 9DN, 1983.

Copyedited by Anna Gourlay
Typeset by Audrey Meek
Proofread by Olive Peat
Cover design by Jan Brown
Photos courtesy of Nils Somby
Printed by The Pitman Press, Bath, U.K.

British Library Cataloguing in Publication Data

Valkeapaa, Nils-Aslak
Greetings from Lappland.
1. Lapps
I. Title   II. Terveisia Lapista pamfletti.
English
948.977   DL971.L2

ISBN 0-86232-155-7
ISBN 0-86232-156-5 Pbk

U.S. Distributor:
Biblio Distribution Center, 81 Adams Drive, Totowa, New Jersey 07512, U.S.A.

Contents

Map 1: Map of the Arctic Area

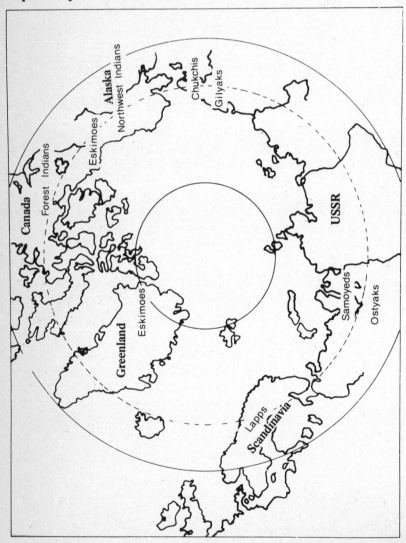

Translator's Foreword

Some readers might find it confusing that a book entitled
Greetings from Lappland then proceeds to talk about people
called 'Samis' who live in 'Samiland', especially since neither
term is to be found in the dictionary. Yet.

Many southern Norwegians claim to be unaware that *lapp* is
a derogatory word in Norwegian. But in the north they know it
all right. And though the word 'Lapp' has no such connotations
for an English-speaking person, they are still there for the people
concerned, and I believe it is a people's right to decide for themselves what they want to be called. For these reasons, I have
chosen to use the terms 'Sami' and 'Samiland', following the
practice of minority and indigenous peoples, and those who
support their right to exist on their own terms.

Similarly, there are many place-names which you will not find
on a map — yet — because I have used Sami names where possible.
I have, however, frequently added the Finnish or Norwegian
equivalent in brackets as a working compromise.

Nils-Aslak Valkeapää wrote the original text in Finnish, though
his mother-tongue is Sami. That was in 1971. In 1979 the text
was adapted for a Norwegian public unfamiliar with Finnish
internal affairs, but the bulk of it remained unaltered, because
most of what Nils-Aslak experienced in Finland has been experienced by 'Norwegian' Samis in Norway (and 'Swedish' Samis in
Sweden). However, several chapters were added to up-date it, so
that *Helsing frå Sameland*, translated by Liv Hatle into New
Norwegian, is considerably different from *Terveisiä Lapista*. I
have worked almost entirely from Liv's translation, and eluci-
dations for an English-speaking (or reading) public mainly take the
form of explanatory footnotes, where we felt a reference was too
obscure for non-Nordic readers, and the author's introduction.

i

So in translating a translation, I hope I have not done any injustice to the original. I am deeply indebted to Liv Hatle, who has given up so much of her time to discuss comparative linguistics (Finnish, Norwegian and English) with me, and to orientate me on Finnish affairs.

The acute reader will notice that virtually all of the pictures have been taken in Norway, during the recent upheavals here, and that the photographer is officially Norwegian (though presently seeking political asylum in Canada). Again, it's all a matter of definition, and who does the defining, and Nils-Aslak Valkeapää and Nils Somby are close friends and neighbours; they just happen to live on opposite sides of a river which the Norwegians and Finns decided to call a boundary. So it seemed rather appropriate that we should illustrate the book (and the point) with Nils' photos.

Beverley Wahl
Oslo, November 1982

Author's Introduction

In your hands you have a book that was originally meant to be an exclamation mark, punctuating a certain moment in time. I wrote *Greetings from Lappland* in Finnish, for the Finns. The title comes from the innumerable postcards which attempt to depict Samiland and the Samis. Almost all of them are dreadful, insulting: non-Samis in thoroughly tasteless, ugly imitations of Sami dress.

I wrote *Greetings from Lappland* in 1970. Twelve years later, summer 1982, the TV sent flashes from the Nordic Conference which was held in Rovaniemi. At that Conference Samis were not mentioned, nor were any Samis present. But they had ushers; young non-Samis, clad in garish imitations of Sami costume. At the time that I wrote *Greetings from Lappland*, my intention was to act as a sort of initiator for discussion. The idea was to write so as to cause controversy, and to create an urge in people to get involved, argue. And a discussion did get started, to some extent.

But today, there have been no noteworthy changes in these matters. Naive that I was, I really believed that the progressive Nordic lands, which involve themselves so readily in Vietnam, Chile, the global situation, had put their own houses in order.

Now I know that the Nordic countries do not acknowledge that we Samis have our rights and our territory. If we try to assert ourselves, the attempt is suppressed, either 'through law and order' or by the use of force. So this little book, which was only meant to be a spontaneous cry of protest, is still fully relevant. And perhaps even relevant in a global perspective, now just as before. Nevertheless, our case is rather special, in that the Nordic countries haven't had to resort to violence, because we Samis are numerically a little people, and because our culture knows of no phenomenon such as 'war'.

But we know that when it's been necessary, and when it is necessary, the Nordic countries use force against Samis.

Greetings from Lappland was at one time going to be translated into Polish. Something went wrong, however, before they managed to bring out a translation, and it still seems rather a pity. The book was translated into Norwegian in 1979, and here's a short extract from the foreword, as a little description of time and place:

> People change pretty fast, Nature as a rule somewhat more slowly. In the short time which has passed since I wrote the book, and until I sit here writing this 'Warning', I haven't changed my ideas to any notable degree. The Sami question is still unsolved. But Nature, Nature has been changed to a frightening degree. Symptomatic. I am sitting at Skibotn (Norway) writing this. The air is already full of noisy insects, roads are full of all kinds of metal, and in the sky lights blink at regular intervals. Thundering and crashing can be heard. About 20,000 NATO soldiers are holding an exercise. I can see a Negro youth stomp through the thick snow on skis, trying to fight his way through the forest. And this is the same Skibotn valley which is presently being razed to provide yet more electrical energy!
>
> One hears opinions for and against the development of the Skaidi and the Alta Rivers in the daily news in Sami. Sami speakers also find it worthy of mention that it has been resolved to raise an elaborate memorial to President Kekkonen at Saivarri, by Lake Kilpis, in the middle of the reindeer pastureland, on Sami ground. And in Swedish Lappland (Norrbotten) nature conservationists have protested again against the resolutions of the local assembly concerning forest felling, and in addition against new mining projects. Ja, ja, these advanced Nordic countries, the conscience of the world, the conscience of the world.
>
> Really highly advanced states carry out genocide without blood, without physical violence. That's how it is.

Originally then, I wrote the book as an introduction to a debate about the Samis' situation in Finland. The text was relevant to the time, and took up a number of topics which were 'in the air' at that point. In addition, there was a good deal of veiled satire. With the passing of the years, new and current matters have arisen whilst earlier ones have been forgotten, including those which were 'in the air' then, which have naturally been completely supplanted by new ravages. For this reason, a good deal of the original text has been left out, but there may still be many things which are difficult to comprehend, seen in a world-wide perspective. I can only ask humbly to be excused. Maybe I'll have to write a whole new book sometime.

All the same, I have to acknowledge the fact that *Greetings from Lappland* has been translated into English. Accordingly, there are a couple of things which should be added.

The figures that appear in the book, including those involving money, are those which were operative in Finland in 1970.

The other thing is, that this is not a scientific work. Every single real doctoral thesis which touches on Sami affairs has as its bounden duty to submit its very own scientific theory on the origin of the Samis — 'where they come from'. We ourselves naturally know where every single person came from, but as a people we don't know whether we 'came from anywhere' But as I said, this book does not aim at being a scientific work. Maybe it will suffice if I say that an average Sami family consists of parents, three children and an anthropologist.

Neither is it my intention to fill this book with current affairs. Those who find their interest awakened will doubtless find their way to the information. For the Norwegian edition I made deletions and additions, and the same has been done for the English edition. I can just briefly mention that the memorial to President Kekkonen was raised, against the Samis' will, on the peak of Saivarri, right in the middle of reindeer pastureland. Thus it· became a symbol of Finnish colonialism. Samiland is full of the great marks of colonialism anyway, you can even see them on the map. One of the greatest will be the Alta power station. This is being built, no matter what the Samis do, no matter how much they point out their rights, even when they point out breaches of Norway's own laws. The approach road to the power station at Alta is finished, and they're starting on the dam. Despite the fact that Samis have gone on hunger-strikes twice, despite the fact that the need for power has been 'calculated incorrectly', despite the fact that large numbers of Norwegian people are opposed to the project.

And the regulation will not be stopped, even though the photographer who has taken the pictures for this book tried to blow up the bridge on the approach road. This attempt was ill-fated; the explosives ignited too early, the photographer lost an eye, and one hand had to be amputated. We must be permitted —

and ought — to look upon this as a symbol.

Norway is causing anxiety and insecurity with her oil wealth. Most of all with the plans for a petroleum pipeline. This pipeline is to go right through reindeer pastureland. The Samis' lands have already been enormously reduced through artificial lakes, mines, mining towns, tourism and roads.

At the moment, militarism is the most disquieting threat. Unfortunately, Samiland is a long way from the capitals, but near 'the clash between East and West'. They want to keep the military areas far away from 'people', close enough to the enemy. And in this case it's not just the Nordic lands which are acting as plunderers of Samiland, but also NATO and the Warsaw pact, in other words the whole Western world. The consequences are, that in the case of war Samiland will be the first and hardest hit goal. What injustice against a people whose culture does not even recognize 'war' as a possibility.

By taking land and water, the basis for making a living is removed. By destroying the basis of livelihoods, one destroys the conditions necessary for living in the traditional manner. In taking land and water, one is taking fish and reindeer. When the reindeer are gone, a vital part of Sami culture is gone.

In making schooling compulsory, one transfers the children to boarding schools. The development of tradition is cut short, the children are taught to think in the Western manner, educated. The bond with Nature is broken, they're taught to be masters over Nature, not part of it. After many years of education, it is difficult for anybody to make contact with Nature in the way one does growing up as part of it. Besides which, after the construction of mines, dams, power stations and military bases, there won't even be very much left of Nature.

Schools have been created to realize the needs and ideals of society. School is for man, and it tries to turn dreams into reality. And of course, those who have power and authority also know what is good for the small and the primitive.

That's how small Sami children also learn to have a nose for money, to think of time in terms of money, of land as money, learn to strive for honour, position and status. Learn that one must have idols, learn to watch idols like new waves, Saturday-night-fevers, follow the top ten, chew gum. Instead of lasso and reindeer horns they've got new toys like machine guns and Hunter jets. That's education, that is.

And education has reached the mountain highlands too. The

first generation of Samis to use snowscooters and cross-country motorbikes are now moving over the highlands. Cars, planes and helicopters make daily life easier. Turf huts and tents have given way to centrally-heated houses equipped with TV and electricity. Money is in the thoughts of reindeer owners rather often, and reindeer are valued in terms of money.

That's education for you.

It doesn't take much to pursue a 'divide and rule' policy against a little people. It helps, too, that the little people have quite another cultural philosophy, so that, for instance, they don't see that it's possible to own land and water, or be the possessor of air. Then it's easy for the 'divider and ruler' to write laws which show that this little people doesn't own anything, that they have no right to exist, and finally, that they don't exist.

Should they manage to exist all the same, then these 'divide and rule' powers emphasize that it's a question of Finnish Samis, Swedish Samis, Norwegian Samis and Soviet Samis. 'Divide and rule' grants scholarships to Finnish Samis, the Nordic countries promise economic support to the Norwegian Samis' central organization, to the Swedish Samis' central organization . . .

The dividing lines which split the Sami people are confirmed in many ways every day.

There is some co-operation between Samis across the borders. But if the Nordic lands build an institution with Nordic funds, then Norway prefers to pay the lion's share, because most Samis live in Norway. And this is only right, seen with Swedish and Finnish eyes. The presupposition is naturally that 'a common Nordic radio station for Samis will be built in Norway. If it gets built'.

This is rather clever, for if all the common Nordic Sami institutions were established in Norway, it's conceivable that the other Nordic lands, Sweden and Finland, won't be very interested in common Nordic institutions at all, especially not Sami institutions. And what sort of Nordic co-operation is that, with everything going to Norway? And the Samis, who feel themselves to be one people, lose hope, and feel that the borders are uncrossable.

'Divide and rule' works, and Samis have been trained to rebound off the borders, just like Pavlov's dogs. They've been conditioned to be Swedish, Finnish and Norwegian citizens. Conditioned to support their 'fatherland'. Taught to shout *'Heija'* if Sweden is winning an ice-hockey match, or *'Eläköön'* if Finland wins the women's ski relay. Of course this is reinforced

by giving rewards, with gold and honour. The good and faithful
are made section leaders, their salaries are raised, holidays and
other goods come their way. And they have complete power to
determine the affairs of other Samis. It goes without saying that
those organizations that promise to be faithful to 'King and
Government' (generally promised in writing in the organization's
statutes) will be pretty sure of getting economic support.

Laws are made by Man, and are based on what Man, culture,
consider to be right and proper. But cultures can be as variable as
the rainbow. Consequently Man's conceptions of what is right and
legal is very divergent. Man is on an equal footing only in death.
And accordingly peoples are also equal only in principle. He who
has might, is right. And it's the laws of the strongest which are
followed. The Samis' cultural philosophy represents the philosophy of natural peoples; that of the Nordic lands, the philosophy
of the West. The Sami conception of justice has been very different from that of the West. Samis constitute in truth only a small
minority in the North. So it's only the Western way of thinking
which the Nordic lands acknowledge in their legal systems.

Whilst the North is taking Samiland piecemeal, it promises at
the same time, almost as a general rule, solemnly and convincingly, that 'What is left belongs to the Samis for eternity'. On
the basis of these laws, which they have made themselves, Samis
have tried, and still try, to seek support, and try their rights
before Nordic courts of justice.

This is virtually futile; the situation is the same as if in the
animal world it was the wolf who made the laws, and the reindeer
pursued his case according to the laws of the wolf, with the wolf
as judge.

Democracy is a fine and beautiful thing. As long as those who
are involved are alike and equal. But if there are different peoples
within the same state, the minorities have no chance to promote
their rights according to democratic rules of the game. Because in
a democracy, only one single majority voice can be decisive, and
the minorities have no chance of acquiring that voice.

There are exceptions that concern those minorities which
imagine that they are the lords of Nature, rulers of the world, the
ones who have power. And weapons. But I don't believe there will
ever be peace in the world as long as there are peoples who feel
themselves to be a people, but who are not allowed to control
their own affairs and their lives. Like people. Like human beings.

But I know that it's not everybody who wishes for peace.

Nevertheless, peoples and cultures are like waves on the ocean of life, coming and going. Maybe that's the meaning of life, that in order to grow one must die.

In an industrialized world, which is like a fisher who is fishing out his lake, and who in addition is poisoning the water, the philosophy of life of the indigenous peoples may turn out to be very important as teaching examples for that world.

Still, the Earth is small, and feels smaller and smaller as time goes by. That's why I'm moved to open my heart, and wish warmth and understanding for all the peoples of the Earth.

For we live and dwell on the same Earth.

I wish you joy and fellowship, with love.

Nils-Aslak Valkeapää
Beaddet 1982

In Western Europe people believe that the land we live in . . .

The Farthest Land

Western culture evaluates other cultures through comparison with itself. Thus foreign cultures are usually viewed as primitive vestiges from a prehistoric age, people with another cultural background are looked upon as primitive beings, and their creative work is consequently called primitive art. Of course, it's a long time since Western culture conceived of the Earth as a pancake, and we're forced to smile at the thought of our childhood.

Ultima Thule is in truth a far-off land. An exotic land of ice, snow and Samis. The cradle of Arctic hysteria. The ice-box of Europe. Blue tinted mountains, a frighteningly long dark period, and fairy-tale, sun-filled summer nights.

At any rate, it's a damn long way from Helsinki.

Farther than to Tenerife.

People who are concerned with social questions ought not to be wholly unfamiliar with the situation in Samiland, that distant dome where people dwell in turf huts and live from hand to mouth under wretched conditions. The arduous living conditions have indeed made these people small and stunted. They are bow-legged from rickets, and soot and smoke have given them squinting, watery eyes. Their hair is straight and black, and they have a dark, reddish skin, which dirt and sunburn cause to appear even darker.

Anybody with inside information knows the district to be a hatchery for out-of-works, which exports its inhabitants to Sweden to seek their fortunes, or south to be domestic servants or manual labourers. Because there's no use trying to keep body and soul together in Samiland. Maybe one could expect a little concern. From spiritually alert and magnanimous people.

Old clothes.

Even a bit of money.

Double insurance to keep the conscience quiet.

'Keep what quiet?'

'But the Samis get aid. All the time.'

'It would be cheaper to move the whole race to the south, then at least it would be realistic to think of jobs with a future for them. The rest could be put into social care. After all, we're one of the most highly developed states in the world.'

'Think before you speak! Is that the way you show your gratitude?'

I try to think, of course. As far as I'm able with my little brain.

Just look how cleverly the land was plundered from us, turned into State land, to be trodden flat by tourists and made into public recreation areas. In order to safeguard themselves completely, they hacked down all the forests, because in de-timbered country there's no basis for any industry other than tourism. Rivers and lakes are regulated so that Nature's own rhythm is upset, and the Samis are made to see who's really the boss. Naturally the State has to emphasize its right of ownership through psychological suppression, by magnanimously selling us back the land in the form of reindeer pastureland. Those small brains must eventually come to understand that the land belongs to the State, and that the Sami is really only a vagrant on the scantily-covered hillsides.

'The Samis — they're a dying race.'

True enough; this race has been condemned for a long time. But sometimes it happens that death doesn't arrive on the exact day predicted as Doomsday.

But they have neither mother-tongue nor fatherland.

And the really cultivated ones tend to put on a snooty look and inquire in astonishment: 'Can you really speak Finnish . . . ?'

I can speak Finnish, unfortunately. Notably better, in fact, than the average Finnish-speaking inhabitant. I am also capable of thinking in Finnish. And writing. Besides that, I'm fair, almost white-haired. I've even studied a bit.

But above all, I can use a lot of foreign words, at least enough for me not to need to say 'Fuck' about everything.

I may not be very tall, but I'm well built, and I have straight legs. I dress colourfully, and what's more I'm sexy. If I put my mind to it, I can converse in Finnish in soft, lilting tones, so it's not to be wondered at that cultivated and intelligent women want to be acquainted with my sexual talents.

'My word, but he's . . . !'

Unfortunately, I chanced to belong to a *primitive* race. My song is a sort of *yoik*.* And I live in such a godforsaken place, where there's nothing: no theatre, no opera, not even inside lavatories.

Arctic Culture

Of course the world doesn't end at the upper edge of the map. Naturally I know that nobody thinks like that . . .

And yet they do think like that. That's just how it seems to most people: beyond the upper edge of the map, in the north, there's nothing, or if there is anything, then it must be on quite another page of the Atlas, and concern a totally different culture, something completely isolated from the rest of the world.

The Arctic region is rather homogeneous. After all, the area in question is quite small if the map is drawn so that the North Pole falls in the middle of the page. Within this circle exist cultures with striking similarities.

This applies not only to human forms of expression, but equally to the plant and animal life. Vaino J. Oinonen relates in his book *Far North in Lappland*, that in Samiland one finds the 'Lapp rose', which is also found in eastern Siberia, North America and Greenland. The same habitats are common to the rhododendron, stitchwort, spiked grass and other plants. The Norway lemming isn't found anywhere else in the world. It's closest relative is the Ob lemming, which occurs on the other side of the White Sea. Not to mention those animals and birds which

Yoik is a form of singing, with or without words, in which the throat is very tense. Faintly reminiscent of yodelling, very similar to American Indian traditional music. To an initiate it can evoke people, landscape, moods . . .

. . . is wild and uninhabited.

are typical of Arctic regions, and which we don't even think about, e.g. hare, reindeer, fox, snow bunting . . .

Implement finds in arctic areas have pretty much the same geographical distribution as Oinonen's examples from the plant life. When it comes to Man, it's not even necessary to turn to history for aid in demonstrating similarities, because the arctic regions still show many common features.

The question of the Samis' origin has of course aroused interest in scientific circles as well. Proof of this lies in the studies which have been made of the East Samis (also known as *Skolt* Samis). As far as I know, various scientific hypotheses have been made about the origin of the Samis, but there's nothing conclusive. Maybe there never will be, either.

Man's capacity for adapting to his environment is unbelievably great. His long voyages, for example, may be more fantastic than the imagination can conjure up. The Norwegian, Thor Heyerdahl, has demonstrated that not even great oceans need be insuperable obstacles. Another proof of this is the feats of the Vikings. Nevertheless, it's easy to think of the Arctic region as something all on its own.

Ethnographists have also concluded that similar external living conditions create similar cultural forms.

The Arctic area is certainly small. The similarity between the races is so great that one cannot avoid drawing comparisons.

The Norwegian Bishop, E. Berggrav writes about *Beaivašgiedde* in Samiland: '. . . in this remote mountain church of ours, I see before me a flock of tanned, bearded, eagle-like faces, reminiscent of Indians. They are reindeer-herders who have driven their sleighs down from the mountain highlands.'

The Arctic races, i.e. the Inuits, American Indians, Samis, and some races in northern Siberia, have such similar life-styles that it is striking.

The *tent*: much the same amongst Indians and Samis. The *lasso*, which the cowboys and gauchos use, actually came to America from Europe. Band-weaving, which is done on a frame, has developed in a remarkably similar way in Scandinavia and amongst the Pueblo Indians in the southwestern part of the U.S.A., and in addition amongst the Aino people.

But the world doesn't end at the upper edge of the map.

Reindeer husbandry in the Old World is a sequel to hunting, an outcome of the fear that the game would come to an end. The Indians continued to hunt because game was so abundant that they felt no need to herd animals. In many places in Australia, Africa, Samiland and in the New World, game has been trapped by means of snares constructed from woven twigs, or stone walls, which gradually taper off and end in a rounded enclosure. This method has been used to trap reindeer in the forest valleys.
An age-old garment is that which in South America is termed

the *poncho*. We still find something corresponding among the Samis in remote areas. They are made of bearskins, and in the Anar (Inari) district are called *sieppuri*. The skin is used in one piece, and if you want to cover the body properly you have to have two skins, one for the front and one for the back. Similar garments are to be found amongst the Ostyaks, Samoyeds, and many Indian tribes in North America. The Inuits have added a hood to the garment, and the Samis have a similar modification in the *luhkka*. The loincloth, which the Indians use, is also found in essence amongst the Samis. The upper part of the stockings, the *stitgat*, has developed from just such a loincloth. *Moccasins* are footwear not used uniquely by Indians, as is commonly believed; on the contrary they occur in large areas of Siberia, and also sporadically in Samiland and other places in Europe. Amongst the Samis the footwear has developed into *kommagar* and *skallar*. (K. Birket-Smith)

The implement culture of the Arctic regions is common to all A good example for comparison is the harpoon tip, which is similar everywhere. Finds from the comb pottery culture also reveal an identical mode of ornamentation. (*Acta Arctica* II)

In North America, Siberia and Samiland, babies are put into a sort of cradle which the mother can carry on her back, fasten to the back of a reindeer, or hang up in the tent — the so-called *komsa*.

Scientific investigators have overlooked the fact that the *komsa* can contribute to the formation of the body, e.g. the head. Attempts have been made to explain the shape of the skull on the basis of racial theories. The literature merely confirms that the Sami body types are different from those of other European races. Certainly the stature of the Samis can, to a certain extent, be put down to living conditions. A harsh environment inevitably leaves its mark. If you study the Indians you can really see similarities. The characteristic features of the Mongolian race are straight, black hair, and prominent cheek-bones. Recent scientific research has established, on the basis of blood-types, that the Samis do not belong to the Mongolian race (and that the East Samis, on whom the research was carried out, are more intelligent than their neighbours . . .)

Humankind often feels an attraction for the unfamiliar, and the same applies to unfamiliar races. In national assembly records from the 1500s, we find comments about the *birkarls'* mistresses in Samiland. They relate how at the *ting* (national assembly) in

Tornio in 1563, Niilo Hannunpoika bought his freedom for a ransom of 46 mark. He had had relations with a Sami woman who had earlier been the mistress of his nephew.

We find such comments in abundance, so we know that the *birkarls** had mistresses amongst Sami women, who for their part had a hand in the property of their menfolk. Thus the Samis couldn't get away with anything when the tax-collectors were on the prowl. This blending of blood cannot have failed to leave its mark on racial characteristics.

'But Sami belongs to the Finno-Ugrian language group . . .'
The language has first and foremost been a practical instrument. So one must realize that the Samis lost a fair amount of the subject matter for their language as they moved northwards, ever closer to the shores of the Arctic Ocean. New things and new necessities of life led to new words entering the language.

Gradually the distinctive racial characteristics have been erased, but basic features have survived. The traits of being quiet, reserved, and individualistic in their way of thinking, are not unique to the Samis. These characteristics are found to just as great an extent amongst other Arctic peoples, along with the tendency to abuse of alcohol and the well-known phenomenon called 'arctic hysteria'.

The present-day problems of the Arctic peoples have arisen from a common source. The robbing and impoverishment of the Indians has aroused protest all over the world, and the conduct of the white usurpers has been condemned. But even though the Samis have been victims of exactly the same sort of suppression, the dominant society has not had similar criticism levelled against it. This may be because they still prefer to keep quiet about the murder, violence and plundering which has taken place in Sami-land, and which has reduced the Samis to a totally insecure exis-tence. The 'withdrawal' of the Samis to the north was not a consequence of the reindeer moving north to new pastures. Far closer to the truth is that the Samis were forced out by others, and had to find new terrain where they could feel to some extent secure. Accounts of peaceful withdrawal are downright lies, used

* The *birkarls* were Finnish merchants who were given special trading privileges in Samiland by the Swedish king.

to cover up the real events. The same stories are also commonly
served up to the major information centres of the world.

The Arctic cultures have more in common than the character-
ization 'primitive'. Their environments have been more or less the
same, but nevertheless, one would have thought that they would
develop in different directions culturally if there had been no
contact at all between them.

Of course, it's possible to find some likenesses between all
races, if you set out to do it. But in the case of the Arctic peoples,
the similarity is so manifest that you can speak of a common
culture which is peculiar to this area.

The music of the Inuits and the Indians can be called *yoik*. The
yoik of both races can be divided into personal *yoik* and religious
yoik, with sub-divisions within these. Just by listening one is
convinced of the similarity.

The same applies to the story-telling tradition. A strange
example is the story which is found over the whole Arctic region,
and which concerns the human being who is descended from
woman and dog. (The term 'human being' naturally applies only
to people who belong to the tribe in question. Many race names
originally meant 'human being'.) The stories have spread from
Asia to both Europe and America. In America we can follow the
traces right down to Guyana. In Enontekiö there is a story about
a Swedish princess who was hunted into exile in Samiland together
with her dog. In due course she bore a child who was the fore-
father of the Samis. That's why the Samis are valiant and clad
like kings. (Samuli Paulaharju (1875–1944): Finnish folklore
researcher and author.)

Samiland

The ancient Romans were already aware that Samiland (Laponia)
existed.

Not to mention all the others who were also aware.

Our people live off reindeer husbandry, farming, hunting and fishing. We were colonized and now are divided between Norway, Sweden, Finland and the Soviet Union.

These people frequented Samiland: Kvens, *birkarls*, Karelians, White Sea Karelians, Danes, Norwegians, Englishmen, Dutchmen.

If only there had been some wealth.

It would have been all right even if there hadn't been very much!

Because they represented more populous and mightier cultures, they were able to set out on their plundering raids. In many places in Samiland there were blazes which no Sami had set alight, and which certainly weren't campfires. The usurpers found an unknown and unique culture which allowed this to happen. In the beginning. Later, this unique culture couldn't manage to stop the violations. Only the occasional *lavrahaš* — a heroic figure in Sami folk-tales — attempted to take up the struggle. But heroes were few and far between, and the rest were weak and lost the fight.

They collected goods, for up to three different States. Sold goods. Offered round alcohol. In the beginning.

The priests of the Lord preached too. *Yoik* was the voice of the devil in man. The devil must be burned with fire or beheaded. By this means one overcame evil spirits. Even an old man of more than 80 years of age was executed because he was irresponsible enough to *yoik*.

The magic drums were smashed in the intoxication of ravaging. God was a stern god, he burnt the vestiges of paganism, removed the totems. So it was a good thing to live for enlightenment and culture. And for the priests. And for the robbers.

Simple wooden gods and fine stone totems had to be destroyed by those in power. Instead, something better was to come, something more magnificent. So we see how development has taken its course: to this day great, beautiful houses of the Lord are rising all over Samiland. They tell in simple language of God's mercy to a folk clad in reindeer skins.

What does it matter if they're expensive. Cold. And what does it matter if the same expenditure could have paid for community halls, helped the poor, built cold-storage units. These are earthly things, and it's the spiritual which matter.

It's so good to be in heaven.

So they burnt paganism. Enlightened people bowed before pictures, lighted candles, and instead of pouring wine on to the fields, as the heathens did, they drank it themselves. Nevertheless, Samiland was a tract nobody really knew too much about. . . . Mighty Sweden was accused of using Sami witchcraft on voyages of conquest in Europe.

Because Samiland was a sort of no-man's-land, and therefore fell into the sphere of interest of several states, immigrants were granted different sorts of privileges. The word of the law which gave the Samis the right to fishing waters and pasture lands remained unchanged, admittedly. But they'd better not stray onto the hay fields of the settlers.

Gradually the Scandinavian countries developed into enlightened States. Amongst the most advanced and best developed in the world. Peoples in these countries were shaken over the colonial policy in other countries, over the plundering and the exploitation.

In the year 1852 the border between Norway and Sweden was drawn up, and in 1889 Sweden was closed off. Finland demonstrated a magnanimous spirit towards her Samis. Like the highly developed country she was, she gave the Samis the right to live in and frequent their old territories freely. It is true that the statutory rights to fishing waters and pasture-land were forgotten.

During those days the Finns had quite enough to do with finding their own identity: we aren't Swedes, we don't want to be Russians — let's be Finns!

One of the best-known pictures from the years of crisis is Edward Isto's painting 'The Assault', which shows the two-headed eagle making an attack on the virgin Suomi (Finland).* It hung secretly on the walls of many Finns.

* Finland's independence was threatened by Russia

Map 2: Northern Scandinavia: Movement of Peoples

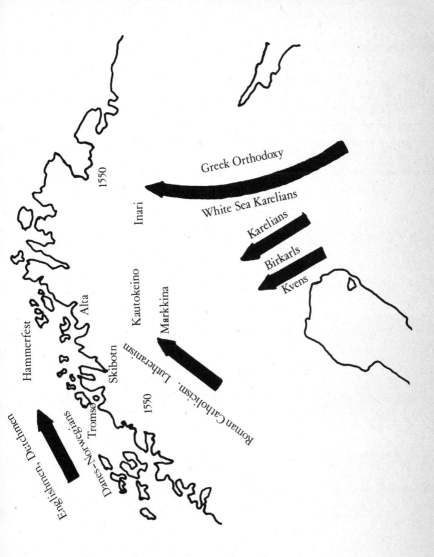

Daccas

There are many *dač̌čas*. Many more than we Samis number altogether. At least in summer and at Easter.

They're usually dressed in black, or at least in grey.

In summer they're bothered by mosquitoes, and strive, cursing, to get rid of them.

In winter they complain about the cold. They have thin stockings and shiny flat shoes on their feet, so I'm not surprised that they complain about the frost.

They are of a better kind than we are. They are friendly to us, and stare at us with curious eyes. As long as we're not in the way. It's worst of all if we are clearly more intelligent than they are.

The smartest thing we can do is be dirty and speak incorrectly. It's also a good idea to be a little foolish. And when they ask us to *yoik* it's best to hum something or other. Because *yoik* is primitive music, and we are primitive people. My word, watch out if you don't feel duty-bound to *yoik* when a *dač̌ča* requests you to, and even worse if it should occur to you to tune up with an aria from the opera Faust by Gounod. The greatest possible grounds for outrage are if it should be performed in German of course. An equally great crime is to sing Schubert's songs for them. Likewise, we are supposed to be greatly astonished by the latest advances in technology. Just say 'oh oh', and so that there can't be the least bit of doubt, widen your eyes, if anybody is kind enough to demonstrate a cigarette lighter. If you get into a car and are given a lift, because the person concerned is going the same way, make sure to press your feet together, and clutch your knees with both hands, though on a bend you can let go with one

---

* A *dač̌ča* is a non-Sami, i.e. foreigner. č is pronounced a 'ch' in 'each'.

hand to hang on to the door, so that you don't get thrown sideways. Be small and afraid, but don't say a word; instead show by your expression and gestures that on the one hand you are terribly frightened, and on the other lost in admiration for the person who can do all this. Oooooh!

I, myself, became acquainted with *dačč̌as* early in life. I went to a school where my teacher was a *dačč̌as*, and for the first year nearly all my classmates were *dačč̌as*. Of course, we only spoke the language of the *dačč̌as* at school. I understood quite quickly

We're a non-violent people. The 'dačč̌a' came with his military violence and colonized us.

23

that they had a fantastic past, because even outside school hours
I used to hear them talk about the good old days.

Later, I noticed that their culture is by nature conservative, and
that the faintest glint of new forms of expression is condemned
as 'the emperor's new clothes'. They are bound so fast to their
established lines of thought that they really experience the fear of
new thoughts physically. God help us, how shameful it must be
to go around in the emperor's new clothes.

At any rate, I listened to long monologues about the heroic
deeds of their forefathers. From time to time I thought that they
certainly seemed to have degenerated rather lamentably.

We were also taught how my own forefathers declined. They
had actually prayed to gods of stone, and sacrificed to them in
the belief that that would give results. People who spread fat on
stones, and set it alight if they didn't get their wishes fulfilled
couldn't be anything but bestial, lost souls.

Of course, I became acquainted with the *dačččas*' way of life,
and observed that now and then they went into a great, grey,
brick house which was cold and damp. There they bowed down
before a picture. I couldn't see any essential difference between
the sacrificial customs of my ancestors and those of the *daččas*.
The *daččas* had merely built the stones into a house, and then they
bowed down before a beautiful picture of a person. And drank
the wine themselves.

And in order to maintain a clear conscience, they go at least
once a year, at the beginning of December,* to the graveyard to
worship their dead. No matter how biting the cold and fog may
be, they will stand there bare-headed and thank their God that it
should be they who triumphed over their enemies, even though it
was obvious that it had to turn out like that, for the *daččas*
believe themselves to be His chosen people. Together with the
Israelites.

Mighty monuments have been raised to commemorate events of
distant times, and especially how the enemy attacked. They have
gone to great pains to organize schooling for their retarded
children. By contrast, some who have come further in their
development, have not received comparable offers: those who are
a little ahead of their times are permitted to get along by their

* Finland's national day is 6 December.

24

own efforts, whether they be children or adults. Besides, new thinking is a manifest danger to the powers that be. There's a certain fear of making new plans: it's just a craze, and we can't afford to get involved in that sort of thing. They don't care to speculate on the future, and won't tie up capital in affairs which may entail expense in the future.

In order to avoid seeing any changes which may arise in due course, they have developed an ingenious solution: they have frozen their language fast. Every single person must know the only correct method of writing, and the degree of one's cultivation is determined by whether one can pronounce a soft 'd'. All new phenomena must of necessity get new names. However, there are two permissible exceptions to this rule: the one is that a really venerable person demonstrates his status by adopting titles in a dead language, and the other is the designations for different parts of the body, which one tries to find names for in the same dead language — to the extent that it might be necessary to speak about such disgusting things.

They're getting advanced, and they have to show that they're great humanists. So they have loud discussions, and make it clear to listeners that they are spiritually liberated, because they are capable of looking at things without prejudice. They hasten to add, however, that of course one has to draw the line somewhere . . . .

The Samis

The Roman historian Tacitus (55–120 A.D.) writes in his book *Germania* about a people whom he calls the *fenni* who lived on the eastern side of the Baltic Sea, i.e. east of the Wizla mouth. This is considered to be the earliest record of the people who are called Samis. In the middle of the second century, Ptolemy of Alexandria speaks in his work *Geographia* of two types of *Phinnoi* people, the one settled by the Wizla, and the other right up in the northern part of Scandia.

The names 'Lappland' and 'Lapp' first appeared in literature towards the end of the 12th Century, when Saxo Grammaticus speaks of *'utraque Lappia'* — 'both Laplands'.

In Norway one still speaks of *Finnmark*, of the *finnemisjonen* (Finnish mission), *finner* (Finns) and means not Finns, but Samis. But the word *same* (pronounced *sah-ma*) is coming into general use. Finlanders are known by the name *kvener* (Kvens), a name which is possibly derived from the word *kainuu*. (Kainuu is a region in Finland.)

In their own language the Samis call themselves *sápmelas̆*. Yet this is only partly true. Especially in the Enontekiö-Kautokeino area, *sápmelas̆* means reindeer-herding Sami. *Meron* means a Sami who lives off what he catches in the sea. *Dálon* is a farmer. *Merra* is someone who lives from fishing but isn't a Sami. *Láddelas̆* is a settler. *Dárru* is a farmer who lives in a fenced-off area. *Dac̆c̆a* originated from the word *danza*, Dane. The latter are thus non-Samis. There are also names which aren't related to race, but to small occupational groups such as merchants, sextons, priests and so forth.

The reindeer-herding Sami has, in truth, been a prince of the mountains; on his wanderings he has seen the world, experienced the cosmopolitan spirit, and lived in harmony with the mountains and enjoyed the freedom they have given him.

Samis now live in Sweden, Norway, Finland and the Soviet

Map 3: Sami Areas of Finland

"" East (Skolt) Samis

== Fisher Samis

We have lived in Samiland since the dawn of time, and we live and dwell here still...

Union. Our number is a matter of estimation. Guesses have been made at anything between 50,000 and 100,000. According to research by the Committee for Sami Questions (1952, pp. 20–30) we number about 36,500, distributed in the following manner:

In Norway about 22,000 people.

In Sweden 10,193 people (1945).

In Finland 2,529 people.

In the Soviet Union 1,920 people (1933).

With the best will in the world, I can't help smiling at these exact figures. Maybe we've been registered by the pedigree system.

The figures show no basis for the talk and predictions about a dying race. There are more Samis than ever before (or so some research workers maintain) and our number has become greater since we have been conceived of as a people.

In Finland Samis only live in Utsjok, Anar, Enontekiö and Sodankylä now, and according to the last census number about 3,700.

Language-wise the Samis of Finland are a heterogeneous group.

In fact, East Sami can be considered a separate language. The fisher Samis or Anar also have a dialect which is very remote from North Sami.

Since the most ancient times, the Samis have been the victims of assault by a series of enemies. Such was also the fate of the Sami settlement around Kemi. A sudden attack from the east was made there. It is also related of Kemijärvi, which in the old days was Kemi Samiland, that in long-distant times the Swedes wiped out two Sami towns here, Riuhtala and Termuslahti. (Jaakko Fellman)*

Innumerable battles were waged against the Russians and the Karelians. Both embarked over and over on voyages of plunder. They killed, looted and burnt all they came across. Thus it is said that their hordes murdered all the inhabitants of Sompio who tried to flee. But there are also stories of Sami victories. Above all, of the leader Lavrahaš, who through unusually great cunning and heroism caused the Karelians to suffer great losses. (Jaakko Fellman)

Before these events, the Finns and Swedes were encouraged by the manifesto of 27th September 1673 to settle in Samiland, in order to increase the population there. In addition they were encouraged to take over waste and unused land, to cultivate fields and meadows in the areas which the Samis, as a result of their way of life, could not make use of, and in addition to make a livelihood from what they could get out of forests, rivers and lakes, but without infringing on the rights of the Samis in their territories. (Jaakko Fellman)

* Jaakko Fellman (1795–1875) — priest (amongst other places, in Utsjoki) and folklore researcher. He preached in Sami, and published various writings in Sami.

Map 4: Sami-inhabited Areas at Various Dates

(a) Scandinavia, circa 0 A.D.

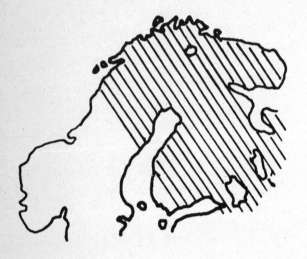

(b) Scandinavia, Today

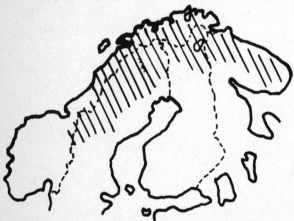

(c) Finland, Various Dates

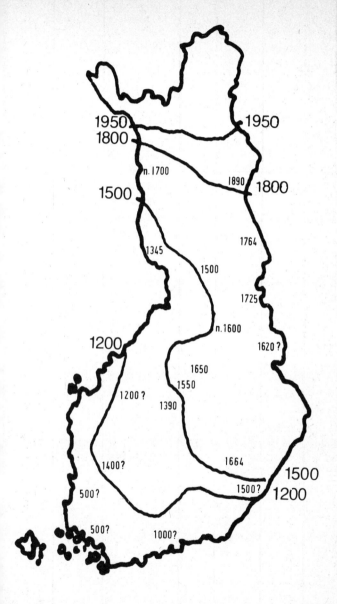

The Tent

Reindeers, sleighs, tents, Samis.

It may be pictures from an ABC book, from a geography book, from a fairy story, or from news-stand literature.

When you add a touch of northern lights, or alternatively nights without sunset, well, you have a fine pamphlet to send abroad; adverts, brochures . . . from Suomi . . . FINLAND, you see!

According to information which the Committee for Sami Questions collected in 1948, three-fifths of the Samis in Enontekiö had moved away from reindeer husbandry, the corresponding figures for Anar and Utsjoki were two-fifths.

The figures ought to be pretty valid today as well. For example, the majority of the Samis in the Utsjoki district live in the Tana and Utsjoki valleys, and they live off a sort of natural economy, most commonly a combination of fishing, domestic animals and incidental income.

The Sami costume has fallen more and more into disuse. Amongst Finnish Samis, it is only in Enontekiö that one finds the Sami costume in daily use. Otherwise the garment tends to be reserved for special occasions.

In Finnish Samiland, it is only the reindeer Samis of Enontekiö who are really nomads, and amongst them the migratory technique has changed in pace with the new demands for efficiency, so that cars and snow-scooters have replaced reindeer teams. Tents are now used only by reindeer herders, because families have permanent dwellings, sometimes even in two places. The houses may well be small, and they are often badly constructed.

Even though it is the countryman's culture which is normally viewed as having conservative influence, amongst the Samis reindeer husbandry is singled out as having a corresponding function. It is through this life-style that the Sami culture is visualized as being preserved and developed.

In recent times, 'Samis' have appeared all over the place. Thus, a whole Sami town may suddenly spring up outside Rovaniemi, as though spirited up out of thin air, only to disappear as soon as the far-travelling guests have got into their planes to fly away, each to his own part of the world.

It's not surprising that the Samis feel bitter sometimes. It wasn't enough that the *birkarls* demanded tax and procured ownership rights over the Samis. Nor was it enough that land and water which belonged to Samis was taken from them. They had to be sucked completely dry, and finally, barren and stony mountain regions were placed at the disposition of the tourist industry. And now they even want to take the only thing the Samis have left — their appearance, which is to become Finland's great draw in tourist advertisements.

I just wonder if there's anything left that can be pillaged. Even the soul can be 'brain-washed'.

The Meat Industry

Reindeer husbandry is one of the most profitable and natural sources of income in Sami districts. Reindeer husbandry does hold a central place amongst Sami occupations, but on pasture lands in the area in question, where there could theoretically be some 100,000 animals, today's technology means that there can be only 80,000 in the same area, and the actual number of reindeer today will stand at about 70,000.*

Despite technology, reindeer husbandry is based on the same principles which held true at the time that nomadism was the rule of the land. It is undoubtedly less elevated to talk of the

---

* Figures are relative rather than substantive.

Reindeer husbandry is one of the most profitable and natural livelihoods in Samiland, but the majority society is interfering . . .

meat industry, if one can speak of reindeer husbandry instead. In the past it was natural for a flock to be composed of cows, calves, and quite a large number of bulls: they all had a function within the system. But we live in Samiland in a motorized age, and reindeer are not much in demand as draft animals, nor to any great extent for the sake of the by-products in the traditional sense. So one can speak of meat-production without batting an eye. That being the case, the cows can make up the major part of the herd, for experience proves that one bull with 50 cows can keep the herd going. By radically changing the composition of the flock, people were able to reduce very considerably the amount of work required for each saleable carcass, especially if the calves were sold the first autumn. The weight of the calves is naturally much less than that of the adult animals, but the number is so much greater, the amount of work less, and in addition it means one saves on pasture. In that way the pasture-land could nourish those animals which really gave returns. In addition, calf meat is of better quality. It's quite obvious that there are animals on the pasture land which eat up the slow-growing moss and give the owner extra work without giving any returns, for disappearance accounts for a fair number of reindeer. It has been calculated that 30% vanish in the course of a year and a half, whilst disappearance of calves amounts to only 15%. If the composition of the herd were based on calculations, a herd of 200 animals would be composed of 180 cows, the rest being stud bulls of different ages. There would still be a reserve. If the average loss of calves was 15%, there would still be 150 calves to sell in autumn.

If you take the average price for a second-year animal as 250 mark, and for a first-year calf as 150 mark, you can do a little calculation.* If you have 200 reindeer, which is quite a respectable number these days, you can according to existing practice, sell about 60 second-year animals (15,000 mark). If you sell calves, you can probably sell about 150 (22,000 mark) and at the same time save work and deliver better quality meat.

Since the pasture area can't be expanded, neither can the total number of reindeer be increased. At any rate, the number of reindeer owners has increased now, and consequently the number of reindeer per owner has declined steadily. When you think of the rise in the standard of living, you're bound to assume that the prospects aren't very enticing for those who are interested in taking up this livelihood. Business and improvement of the strain ought also to have headed for better times. Clearly, it should be in the interests of the economy of the commune to make the most possible out of reindeer husbandry, and one would therefore expect the ruling powers to show some interest in this occupation.

The battle for a place in the sun will doubtless soon be under way in Samiland too. I believe it's foolish to let reindeer fall into the hands of those who don't need them. There are also many things which indicate that reindeer owners must pay more attention to improving the strain, to the use of snow-scooters, scientific investigations and business methods. In addition, the reindeer husbandry organizations must function as trade unions and pressure groups.

* Prices as in 1971

Nomadism

If I restricted myself to a purely technocratic presentation it would give an extremely one-sided and incomplete picture of reindeer husbandry. The tendency to cold calculation within reindeer husbandry has come to the Sami culture from the outside, mainly from the *dačča*, and through the reindeer pasture system. All the economic principles of capitalism apply in full force there: more, faster, more easily. For the Samis themselves, reindeer-herding is a way of life, a philosophy. From the writing desk, nomadism can seem pretty underdeveloped and primitive, but then a writing desk is also a rare commodity in the mountains.

If the meat industry should function to maximum capacity, there would immediately be a danger of impoverishing the pasture-land. Where the meat industry uses calculation, nomadism uses feeling and heart. Throughout the centuries it has developed more than just one occupation; it has created the core of a culture. Perhaps there will come a time when the way of life which reindeer-herding is associated with will be the highest and most advanced!

Scientific research workers have had to acknowledge that the traditional methods of reindeer husbandry are the most appropriate in the long run. Methods suitable for an effective meat industry over a short period, are not always equally suitable when the health and power of resistance of the animals are taken into account. In critical periods it can be an advantage to have some older and larger animals which can break their way through the snow crust so that the herd can get to new pastures.

And besides, the reindeer is not just a meat producer in the nomadic life-style. Meat production isn't even its chief function. Each reindeer has its task and, amongst other things, is a means of transport. One which doesn't pollute.

In nomadism, all parts of the reindeer are employed. Clothes for people. Bedclothes. The innards become blood sausage. Even the head is used for food, and the marrow-bone is real feast provender. The largest guts are used for vessels and containers. Actually it's only the stomach which is left as a delicacy for the wild animals. The dogs also need their share, and they're an important element in the pattern of life.

The meat industry is faced with problems. The slaughterhouse is having difficulty finding a place to dispose of the heads and hooves. Migration itself, this wandering from one place to another, also has its function. It has prevented too many demands being made on the susceptible countryside, either by people or by animals. This can be food for thought in an age when there are ever more cottages and other permanent settlements!

Migrating with the reindeer has been an important factor in the development of Sami culture. The wandering life is a life of freedom. There are no chains binding us to the same place. New landscapes and new perspectives also liberate the mind and thoughts. There can be no doubt that mode of living also affects personality. It may be therapy.

The ambulatory settlement may well have stimulated growth and the countryside. In many places this can clearly be seen.

Nomadism captivates me first and foremost through its philosophy. By being a part of Nature, Man shows respect for Nature. The fact that the Sami culture has extended reindeer-herding more into a way of life than a means of living is undoubtedly bound up with this 'part-of-Nature' way of thinking. That reindeer husbandry has subordinated itself to the principles of the meat industry is a step towards the usual, commercial mode of thought, which follows on from the idea 'Go out and make all the animals and birds your subjects'. In other words, 'Man is lord over Nature'. This ideology has landed the whole planet in a state which is optimistically called a 'depression'. If one examines the true state of the world ever so little, amongst other things the food supply, one sees that it isn't merely a matter of 'depression'.

Since the nomadic life — in all its primitiveness — has become a part of Nature and maintains a peaceful coexistence with it, surely that gives every ground for regarding this mode of living as advanced? It should be especially important to encourage such a way of life bearing the world situation in mind, and this philosophy could be a model for the society which is enveloped in 'depression'.

In this context one inevitably comes to the school system. The idea is surely that schooling is there for the people, and the society we live in. It is unfortunate for reindeer-herding that children are

In Sami culture, reindeer husbandry has become more a mode of life than a means of living.

taken away from the environment at an early age. Not only are they removed from the mountains, they are also transplanted to a different environment and taught new ways of living, with the result that they develop a lack of respect for both the countryside and the herder's life. From an ecological point of view this is unfortunate, for it is certain that their view of the countryside will be altered in the course of their school years. This causes adaptational difficulties later.

Since society has no teachers who can teach nomadism, one solution would be for the parents to take care of this instruction, at least during the child's formative years. Not only that, but society must naturally pay for this teaching. That should be self-evident.

The Snow-Scooter

We don't have thousands of reindeer. Not even those who *really* have reindeer do. Most people have less than 200.

Most of us have a family. Parents. Wife and children. To tell the truth, the flocks of children aren't as large as you're led to believe either. Most of us have a house. A little one, something like this: two rooms, a wood-oven, and an outside lavatory. Many of us have two houses. Many families have cars.

From the *dačča* we learned to drink spirits, once upon a time.

And then we have snow-scooters.

All of us.

They used to say wisely, that if ever there was an end to wolves and thieves in Samiland, it would be the end of the reindeer too. By this they meant to say that reindeer owners couldn't be bothered to herd their animals if there wasn't at all times an imminent danger that the animals would vanish.

In eastern tracts there are wolves.

Here in Enontekiö they only appear sporadically.

But we have snow-scooters.

All of us.

Man in his wisdom created the snow-scooter.

Man in his foolishness took it out to the reindeer herd.

It ate more than the wolf.

We can only sell reindeer to a value of about 15,000 mark annually. One snow-scooter costs about 4,000 mark.

The snow-scooter is in daily use from the beginning of October to the end of April.

We drive it on average for two winters, and during that time we use at least 2–4 belts (at 500 mark each). Not to mention all the minor parts and nuts and bolts (at 100 mark) plenty of which go each month. Then when we trade in the scooter, after two years, we get about 1,000 mark for it. During one winter, we use about 1,500 litres of petrol, and road tax is included in the cost, even though it's not legal to drive on the roads with snow-scooters. So anybody can work out quite easily that all in all, it doesn't pay us to have snow-scooters.

But we can't afford to be without, for without snow-scooters, we're soon back to being old-fashioned reindeer-herders, the whole lot of us.

The snow-scooter is employed daily from the beginning of October until the turn of the month April–May.

To tell the truth, our ears can't stand this mode of travelling, and all reindeer herders have suffered markedly impaired hearing during the course of recent years. We've started complaining about our backs. The small of the back is particularly vulnerable. In addition we have discovered that the Creator did not intend the knee to be employed as a heel: for we often have to kneel to drive because there are small differences in size between scooter models.

Herders often get impatient when they feel they're moving too slowly, and then the reindeer get to experience the marvellous sensations which the motor affords man: so even the wildest animals have to bow down to the fact that a machine is a machine. Of course, the reindeer get thin through this sort of travelling, but at any rate they are forced to admit that Man is the boss in the countryside as well.

Nor do the tourists get a smile out of us when they want to take photographs of the herd in spring when calving time is approaching. It can't be done without the aid of a snow-scooter.

So we all have snow-scooters.

Nobody can afford to be without.

In some families there are several herders.

That means they have to have several scooters as well.

Wolves

We feel ourselves to be subject to the pot-bellied powers that be.

Nobody ever asks our opinion.

At times the attacks that conservationists come up with against nomadic Samis can seem quite incomprehensible. What beats everything is that on the infrequent occasions when they come across a wolf in the south of the country, though it's not actually doing anybody any harm, it's hunted by a battalion of a thousand

* Wolves are the greatest enemies of reindeer, consequently of Samis. But conservationists get upset if Samis shoot them.

Traditionally, wolves are reindeer husbandry's greatest enemy, but the majority society is a greater enemy . . .

men. And the man who lets off the decisive shot is the great hero.

Where is the soul of the conservationist sleeping then?

Maybe he's sweating over a manuscript for the magazine where they write that north of Oulu nobody can read.

I know conservationist ideas well. Was active there myself. Even a member of the Association for the Conservation of Nature, right until I read somewhere that here in the north we are all illiterates.

A human being who lives in and off the countryside is an important part of it. He must adapt himself to Nature, and as a rule Nature has forced him to do so. The law is simple. He who doesn't adapt, doesn't survive.

The pot-bellies can walk right past you, without even noticing that there's anyone else there. Maybe that can be interpreted as meaning that the local inhabitants have advanced so far in adaptation that they have become invisible.

Or maybe the reason is that the pot-bellies lack sensory

capacities.

The case has undeniably been registered. By both parties.
The dispute is really about who is to suffer for the disadvantages.
In the end it boils down to a question of economics.

> Conservationists, as friends and protectors of life, can be
> criticized for having an outlook which is divorced from
> reality. They go around under the impression that the life of
> a kestrel or some rare marsh-creature is just as valuable as
> people's standard of living, the development of society, and
> the whole machinery. Their demands are often totally
> unrealistic. From time to time the idea of an enormous
> national park arises. I remember Bishop Olavi Kares pro-
> posing the idea of a national park to me, patterned on the
> Yellowstone, with bears, wolves and wolverines. This park
> was to lie in the Kuusamo-Salla tracts. This great humanist
> and spiritual figure emphasized that he was a layman in these
> matters; but he was very enthusiastic over the idea. I was
> nevertheless irreverent enough to cast doubts on the possi-
> bility of breeding a strain of bear which would set up lairs
> within view of tourists' car windows. (Vaikko Huovinen.)*

Conservation in Samiland seems to consist merely of various
forms of restriction and prohibition. If you exclude the little
which has been done for breeding fish, all positive work aimed at
improving wild strains has been totally neglected. The right to hunt
is sold to anybody at all, as long as they have a licence to handle
a gun.

In autumn you come across the strangest people in the most
unexpected places, out to hunt. Since ptarmigan hunting is desig-
nated a source of income in Sami areas, and since hunting com-
bined with fishing actually comprises a means of livelihood, this
practice seems very negative. In addition come all those hunters
who employ hunting dogs, and who assure you that this dog is
the most obedient and most intelligent in existence. They talk of
'Him'.

* Vaikko Huovinen, (1927–   ), Finnish forester and author of
literary works. (Translator's note.)

But this well-behaved dog, 'He', runs after reindeer and causes considerable damage.

In Samiland people have traditionally shot waterbirds in spring. This is now forbidden. But it is still done, despite the ban.

I'm not a person who's fond of hunting. But I have felt that this ban is an injustice to the local inhabitants. The ducks could have been a valuable supplement to provisions. Now this source is gone, or only exists in secret. One can easily assume that this practice still exists, because people get around laws if they find it vital enough. It's difficult to give a logical explanation for the ban here in the north, and correspondingly difficult to motivate people to be obedient to the law. Waterbirds are usually plump and in good condition when they travel northwards in spring. They're also shy and manage to escape easily. So you'd expect a good proportion to survive even if they were hunted, because one takes waterbirds only for one's own use. They're not put up for sale. When the birds lay eggs and broods, it gets thin and the meat deteriorates, to such an extent that it may be inedible. It's not very likely that people will go hunting to procure spoilt meat for their own tables.

In autumn you see flocks of ducks. The young collect in small lakes, and when the hunting season begins on 20 August, they are usually still not capable of flying. The lakes may be full of them, but it's not much fun shooting the poor little things, as though off a tray.

When the birds have grown somewhat bigger and fatter, they head for the south, so nobody here goes duck-hunting in autumn.

In spring, by contrast, they do.

And of course there's a certain added thrill in it, since it's illegal.

Is the State inciting illegality against its better judgement?

Karl IX received complaints from the Kemi Samis, especially those who lived in Peltojärvi, Kittilä, Sodankylä, and Maanselkä, that the birkarls and some of the farmers had caused damage and had encroached on the fishing waters. On the basis of this grievance the king extended written protection to the Samis in question, but in the year 1638 it transpired that in spite of this, the farmers in Kemi had fished and hunted and cleared the land by burning the overcover of Kemijärvi. (T.I. Itkonen.)

In the year 1642 the Kemi Samis approached the governor
with bitter complaints that many rich farmers sho have
fertile land in Savo and Oulu encroach on our lands across
the borders, and descend on our fishing waters, especially
in Kemijärvi and other remote areas. They entice our youth
into their service, and when they get old and frail they chase
them away, so that they're reduced to begging and face
death by starvation. They also employ violence and other
injustice against our people. (T.I. Itkonen.)

In 1584 the border between Sonkamuotka (now Muonio)
and Enontekiö was made the boundary between the farmers
of Tornio and the Samis of Suonttavaara. The Samis had
already been forced out of Muoniojoki. (T.I. Itkonen.)

Karl XI passed a law in 1673 — and another in 1695 —
concerning settlement in Samiland. The new settlers were
exempted from tax for 15 years (in Finnish Samiland the
practice was 25 years) and from all military service. In
addition the Samis' rights should be considered [nothing was
said about in which way]. Haphazard guidance lines were
given in the royal regulation of 1749. There it was stated that
injustice must not be practised against those [meaning Samis]
who on account of the new settlers were losing places they
had formerly used for trapping and fishing, or which they
had employed otherwise than for agriculture. Because the
Samis hunted all game of value and paid tax for the right to
hunt, the new settlers were not allowed to hunt further
than five kilometres outside their dwelling places. In practice
this law had no effect. (T.I. Itkonen.)*

* T.I. Itkonen (1891–1968). Studied Sami language and culture
in the north and on the Kila peninsula. Collected Sami folklore
and studied Sami mythology.

The President

Mr President!
Most revered legislatory body!
Respected conservationists!
True humanitarians!
Cultural elite!

I approach you humbly, trusting in your unfaltering sense of justice, your search for the most basic truths, and your desire and promise to right historical wrongs. If you will allow me, I propose the following:

Conservation of nature is one of the most important activities a reflecting person can occupy himself with, with a thought for the countryside and the future. Samiland represents a type of landscape which is beginning to be a rarity in the world. Perhaps this has been realized, because nature reserves have been set up, and others are being planned. Lemmenjoki Nature Reserve has been extended so as to cover a corresponding area on the Norwegian side.

I propose that the Nature Reserve be extended to include the whole Sami area, i.e. Utsjoki, Inari and Enontekiö communes, and in addition parts of Sodankylä commune.

In addition I suggest that the Samis who live within this area should have the right to pursue their traditional livelihoods such as reindeer husbandry, trapping and fishing and berry gathering. Plans should be made to set aside space for extending settlement

* Kekkonen

areas. Otherwise all construction except that which the Samis need to pursue their livelihoods should be forbidden.

The touring area which is already in use, must continue to be available for such purposes, but only within clearly defined areas, and only permitted routes must be used. I presuppose here that this traffic doesn't damage the countryside or impede the economic life of the local inhabitants. In this way we could develop an environment which is an impressive testament to all the coming generations in the world.

From a moral point of view, the area belongs to the Sami people, so the expedients outlined above would merely be a confirmation of historical facts. The area would thus again come to belong to the Samis, as it did in earlier times, in the Swedish-Finnish period.

The rights of the non-Samis should be restricted to the present situation, in conformity with the prevailing property assessment system.

With all respect for such precious values as humanism, justice and human value, I ask respectfully that my proposals be taken seriously, and that they become a reality.

And now I'm waiting with interest to see what steps you'll take.

Pättikkä, Finland's National Day 1970
Nils-Aslak Valkeapää

Lord of the Forest

The Department of Forestry can no longer work in peace. That is naturally the least price they could expect to pay for their activities.

Resistance from both conservationists and the general public is based on a spontaneous reaction against the neglect shown for conservation of the countryside and for aesthetic considerations. Biologists have pointed out the dynamic harmony in the forests, where countless living and lifeless factors are in a constant flux of interaction, and if one of these factors is disturbed, the result can be a reaction so complex that not even the experts can explain it completely. One result is well-known, and that is that in cleared areas it is sometimes too moist, because the forest no longer absorbs and transpires moisture, and sometimes too dry, because the sun has too free access and bakes the earth. It has also been claimed that forest-felling in Samiland has affected the macro-climate, but more reliable is the information which indicates that the climate has got colder. This factor has come like a blow from fate, and has hindered the growth of forest in the northernmost parts of the country. (Veikka Huovinen.)

It has officially been maintained that these cleared areas aren't very extensive. But this claim is false. In northern and eastern Finland at least there are certainly enormous cleared stretches, which are only broken by narrow forest belts here and there. If you stand and look out over such cleared stretches, you see that they extend as far as the eye can see and further. (Veikka Huovinen.)

Thus you see the results of an undertaking.
Nevertheless, only the visible results.

The nomadic Samis have been robbed of virtually any chance to pursue reindeer husbandry in the forest regions. Reindeer owners have to reduce the number of their animals steadily, and nature-lovers and foot tourists, for whom it is vital to be able to wander freely in field and forest, are banished to areas without a single tree. The game disappears, likewise animals which are adapted to a forest environment. Then, when to crown it all the cloudberry marshes are drained, and the berry fields are ploughed, folk have completely lost the resource which the countryside represents. (Martti Linkola.)

Next to the mountain highlands, the extensive forests are the most important pasturelands for reindeer. The modern methods which are employed in forestry have markedly altered the countryside. The cleared flats lie there,

completely bare, or with some dry stubs, mile after mile,
until they disappear over the horizon. Many of these areas
were supposed to be renewed by the 1950s, but they are
still lying there, waiting to be planted.

Nevertheless, this is only a sample. The next operation
was accomplished by the great forest machines. The cater-
pillars put their snouts to the earth and transformed the
even forest floor into the sheerest tangle. Stripping was cut
out, like all the other old methods. More machines, and a
greater degree of effectivity. Ploughing is the keyword in
modern forestry. The forest floor is torn up in long gashes,
so that it becomes as good as impassable. Anybody who tries
to get through is stopped by clods and roots and uprooted
brush. This can safely be called razing. Even in summer dead
silence reigns. If the Creator gave us the Earth to live on,
he certainly didn't intend this. Clearing and ploughing are
the greatest encroachments into the wilderness since the
ice age. (Urpo Häyrinen.)

So much for the experts and the conservationists.

One encroachment has given way to the next; there's no point
trying to count them up.

Löka and Porttipahta: artificial lakes.

My heart weeps blood (excuse the theatrical expression, but it's
pretty near the truth): at the bottom of the basin lie trees, untouched countryside. Then when the terrain is flooded, moss and
other growths float to the surface and lie bobbing on the waves.
The reindeer huddle together, floating like islands on the water.
They're rescued if the Lord wills it. The big bosses may allow
it, but they don't help. Treetops stick up from the surface of the
water and are witness to the fact that there was once a forest
here, and still is: submerged. The nomadic Samis of the Sodankylä
tract had to search for their reindeer all over Finnish Samiland
after the razing of their pasture-land.

Electric power is important. I see. Of course it's claimed that
atomic power is a better solution. But it's not very amusing to
know that electricity is more expensive right by the power plant
than in the built-up areas in the south. Power development and the
forestry policy seem to go hand in hand, from devastation to
devastation, so we can only assert that all is in the hands of the
Lord.

Urpo Häyrinen wrote as follows in autumn 1967:

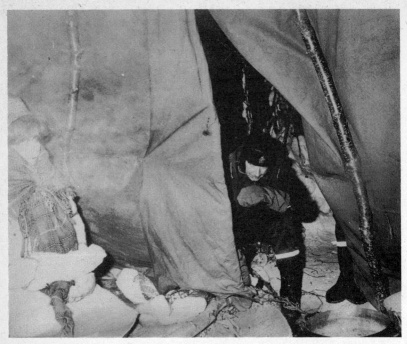

My heart weeps blood when the Vikings come to rob us of our land.

I have examined the damage to various ploughed areas in the north. During ploughing, one third of the forest floor is spared on average, but when half of this is covered by debris from the felling, what it comes down to is that clearing and ploughing together spell total devastation. Of course the idea is to replant the ploughed up areas, but to date I have only seen new planting in two regions. Such incursions obviously have serious consequences for the animal life. Reindeer have great difficulty in passing through ploughed areas, and avoid them as much as they can.

The nomadic Samis have experienced the way this forest management has reduced the supply of winter fodder, causing deaths due to starvation during the spring. Debris from felling obstructs the growth of moss, and drainage is carried out in the bogs and damp forest floor, just where the reindeer find most of their food in summer. Knowing how slowly the forest flora develops, and how long it takes plant life to adapt to the environment, it's easy to work out how

long-lasting the damage due to this activity can be for reindeer pasture-land. Calculating roughly, you can say that a
cleared and ploughed area is worthless to reindeer husbandry
for several decades to come.

The Salmon

The salmon has always been a sort of king of the fishes. This has
always been so owing to its beautiful shape and colour, but it has
never been king to the degree that it is at present.

Samiland can appreciate the legend about the salmon. About
the salmon and about Samiland.

Maybe it's enjoyable for some.

The legend, I mean.

In addition this valuable fish is only found in the Utsjoki water-
course in Finland. By the western border the salmon doesn't swim
up the rivers, or only now and then, when the flood waters are a
bit too high. Salmon usually remain in the nets at Bottenvika and
in the salmon dams by the river mouths.

I.e. just like in the Tana River.

There are umpteen stories about salmon, especially the one that
got away.

Stories of Samis leading someone up the garden path: high
prices charged for the rowing, expensive boat-hire, and on top of
it all they were led completely astray, to places where there was
no earthly chance of finding any fish.

Fishing is an important means of livelihood for Samis. At
present in the form of rowing tourists. It would be nice to take a
little salmon home, too, but the number of fishermen is increasing
all the time.

In summer the place teems with intrepid tourists. They swarm
up the spine of Mount Háldi. The books describe just how difficult it is to crouch behind a rock when the mosquitoes are out in
force.

The rivers are full of otters. The camping places and adjacent

The buoddu, *our ancient method of fishing, provides the people with salmon. The Finnish sports-fishers would like to see it forbidden . . . for their fibre-glass fishing rods to be used in their leisure time.*

areas are full of tin cans and spirit bottles. Irritating people. Act as though they own the world. Just ask them if that's not how they see it. And anyway what is a native worth: they come and try on our clothes, gape and peer, carry out a complete physical examination in sheer wonderment over how interesting we are. They'd like to put our balls on the scales too.

But when they realize that some of us are better informed than they are, there's an immediate outcry: 'But you're just not genuine!'

They're bold wanderers. Experts on nature.

Fishermen.

And the fish bite. Naturally one can't blame the tourists because the fish are coming to an end, but maybe they're the straw that broke the camel's back. Moreover, the law lays down that tourists may not fish with nets. Tourists don't fish illegally, fishing licences are sold here there and everywhere. It's just that I haven't seen the income from the sale of licences go towards the maintenance of the fishing waters.

At any rate, Samis haven't noticed any benefits from this business.

If there should ever be question of dividing up the fishing rights, the Samis will stand there without any protection at all in relation to the tourists.

The fish-breeding which is in progress in Samiland is not benefiting the northernmost parts, at any rate. In recent years fry has admittedly been placed in some waters, but in far too small quantities for there to have been any results worth mentioning.

The Tourist

Drives a car. Fast. Curses the mosquitoes in summer and the snow in winter. Enjoys the company of his whisky bottle. Is discontented, imagines everyone else to be there just to wait on him. Believes that he's doing the people in the place a favour, what's more. Maybe leaves money. Has the right to push his way into people's houses and ask anything whatsoever.

Of course there's money in it. For some.

And naturally it's the business of the future.

With all due respect to those who are trying their luck in the tourist industry. It's not that.

I'm still moved by concern to inquire: Has anybody worked out what tourism costs at all?

I'm a reactionary of course, but I must be allowed to ask at least.

I haven't even been thinking of putting a brake on tourism.

But I put the question humbly forward all the same.

Maybe one could reserve an area for tourists, where they could let themselves go. In a region where it wouldn't hinder the

local inhabitants in their livelihoods. Tourism would naturally be
a source of income then. I don't have anything else in mind.

I know only too well that I can't slow down the development
of tourism. That was the last thing on my mind.

But those who have power and prestige could plan for this
remote country in an appropriate manner. A little bit for everybody. Except in Samiland. There the Samis ought to have the
right of veto, at least outside the built-up areas.

> *For a long time, the greater part of what is now East Karelia
> had a scattered Sami settlement. St Laza, who founded
> Äänisjärvi monastery at the end of the 1300s, said himself
> that he worked amongst the Samis and the Chudes.*
>
> (T.I. Itkonen.)

> *The* birkarls *practised hunting, fishing, animal husbandry and
> trade. They were committed to supplying the Samis with
> commodities. They also practised tax-collection on the basis
> of their household, each and every one of the Samis whom
> they personally owned. Each* birkarl *had a large number of
> Samis from whom he demanded tax, and they were passed
> down through the family through inheritance.* (T.I. Itkonen.)

> *It is nevertheless recorded that in the year 1615, in the Sami
> town of Suonttavaara, in the Tornio region, where there had
> previously been 15–20 taxable Samis, only five persons could
> be found, since the* birkarls *had forced them out of the area.*
>
> (T.I. Itkonen.)

> *A Sami was liable for taxation as soon as he was capable of
> drawing a bow and going hunting, which was reckoned to be
> at the age of 15.*
>
> *In some places further south in Finland, it looks as though
> there were also Samis under private ownership, in the same
> way as under the* birkarls. *Thus we learn that to the Kantala
> estate belonged squirrel hunting areas, fishing waters, and
> Samis. In the year 1454 the* birkarls *of Luulaja and Piitimi
> were accused of treating as their subjects some Samis who
> came from Häme and who paid tax directly to the crown.
> But the* birkarls *could prove that they had been given the
> Samis by their companions in Häme.* (T.I. Itkonen.)

> *Double and treble taxation naturally put a great strain on the
> unfortunate Samis, and they were afraid of the tax-collectors.*

*They were most afraid that the birkarls would seize the best
pelts. Samis often fled to the neighbouring states out of fear,
but the tax-collectors had the right to hunt up the fugitives
and demand tax from them if ever they found their new
abode. (T.I. Itkonen.)*

*Norway's laws? Samis' rights! Hunger-striking on the National Assembly
building's steps — in the tourists' capital city.*

Yoik

A while back, *yoik* was regarded as sinful. At times folk were condemned to death for *yoiking*, because *yoik* and drums were the pathway to hell, one way of making contact with the devil. I happened to be born late enough not to be executed. Nevertheless I have been throttled spiritually. Condemned to hell. It was the believers who came up with this notion, since *yoiking* could also accompany intoxication. In my case the crime was that I was distorting an ancient culture because I started using musical instruments, and renovated *yoik* ever so slightly. It was a manifestation of Sami nationalism.

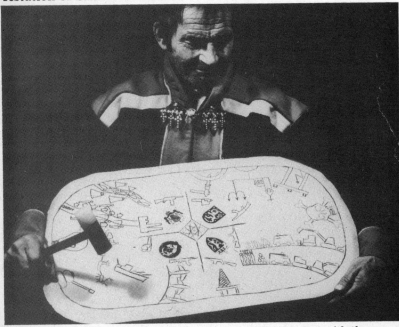

Yoik — *our music* — and drums were a way of making contact with the spirits.

Today I'm doing fine. The young Samis support me. They have accepted me and my way of *yoiking*, they have accepted new ideas. I would have finished with anything related to *yoik* long ago if I had had to function like a tape recorder or a gramophone record. Sheer reproduction would feel like a strait-jacket to me. The situation has altered staggeringly fast. When I think back, I can't imagine many youngsters have experienced such great upheavals during their lifetimes.

Even if I'm being a bit self-important now, it's evident that changes have occurred right down the line, both spiritually and materially. Whether the developments mean progress and improvement, well, I'm not the right one to answer that. I just maintain that a living culture can never stand still.

I am genuine, but I don't want to be genuine in the sense of petrifaction. I want to create new things, I want to live in the culture I was born into, and I shall let myself be influenced by the currents of the times.

Those who speak of races, of pure races, speak rubbish.

Those who speak of preserving a culture are airing their views without realizing that their prattle is absurd.

Everything I do, I do on my own premisses. What I call my art is anchored in the mountain highlands and the people who live there. My people can evaluate everything I do; if they accept it, that's fine. If not, I'm a spiritual refugee from a country which doesn't exist. Each and everyone is alone in his art. Each human being is, through his life, an organic part of the culture he belongs to, whether consciously or unconsciously.

When people are so keen to make Samis into museum pieces — live in tents, herd reindeer — then something is wrong somewhere. When in addition to that they want Samis to reproduce old things which no longer have any practical function, it's not very stimulating to do anything. This eagerness to keep an eye on folk and keep them 'genuine' seems revolting. Just as though everything which was done in the past was good, and nothing can be improved upon, and people aren't capable of creating anything completely new.

It also seems dubious when the Samis become aware of their culture only after the preservation experts have become interested in homecrafts, and demand that they be thus and thus. Once rules and regulations start coming in, the decline will soon be underway too. The sign of a living culture is precisely flux and constant change. It seems as though the adherents of preservation want to press our culture the way one presses plants, in order to admire them later in a herbarium.

Art

The artist is always alone in his art.

Talkers there are in plenty, who clap you on the shoulder, buy you drinks and shower you with opinions and points of view. Nevertheless, the artist has to struggle alone with his art. It is both physically and mentally tiring. At the same time, the artist often has to live in a state of opposition to other people, because creation is often simultaneously a breach with old conventions. Ordinary people don't like to be disturbed, they don't like to be budged in their view of life. People need security and are on guard against anything new.

When you read the biographies of artists, you can't avoid not noticing how difficult this struggle can be. When conditions for artists are so hard in the wealthy part of the world, one may wonder how it is to be a Sami and an artist.

Only in recent times have we realized that there are borders which separate people. On the other side of the river, another language is taught; in corresponding schools, the world is carefully filtered. Contemporary affairs, history, ethics, are passed through one 'neutral' sieve here, another 'neutral' sieve there, and through the NATO sieve over there.* There's barely any instruction in our mother tongue, and the philosophy of our own people is denigrated and stamped underdeveloped. As the great ideal they also introduce such dangerous things as technology, maximization, and effectivity into the Arctic environment. The forces which rule Nature!

When we speak of Sami art, it's worth remembering that we have our own cultural background, but that we have adopted a

* i.e. in Finland, Sweden and Norway respectively!

quantity of words from neighbouring nations — words like war
and hell — and art and artists.

Sami culture is a speciality, a way of surviving in the Arctic
climate, a part of this environment. Our philosophy is based on
living in such a way that we are constantly in harmony with
Nature. We have to show respect for mountains and climate,
thunder, wind, fog, sun and rain. With this philosophy of life,
setting up lasting memorials to ourselves has been irrelevant. It
hasn't been necessary to say, 'I'm the greatest, I leave an ever-
lasting mighty visiting card behind me, and I will be remembered
for ever, à la pyramids of Egypt.'

It's not like that.

Walls used to be unknown in the Sami culture, and so nobody
hung up pictures. When you think how heavy books are, they're
not the first thing one puts into one's supply bag when one
heads for the mountains to herd reindeer. And anyway, this

The artist is always alone in his art.

knowing the ABC is a doubtful asset. You don't get to learn your own language,* and the foreign one you don't understand — or don't want to understand.

When you consider that houses are a product of recent years, and that electricity is an even newer phenomenon, perhaps you can understand that LPs don't make particularly cheap pictures, either, especially when there's a round black stiff thing pushed into the jacket, which you can't put to any use.

But Sami culture is not strange to art. Far from it. Art has been a part of daily life for the Samis, something one doesn't even talk of in isolation. Real folk art. As is only natural, Sami art is part of the philosophy of life. So it is something which goes together with the countryside, harmonizes with and echoes it, without leaving a mark behind.

Just look at the costume, the *yoik*, and the story-telling tradition. I want to stress that beauty is so important to Samis that our whole way of life becomes art. Speech is music, rich in metaphors and symbols. The landscape we live in, and our wanderings there. Isn't it beautiful to behold? Don't wind, water-falls, fire and *yoik* represent a music which has no beginning and no end? Let us hope it will never cease.

This is how I see it. Art as an isolated phenomenon is unknown to the Samis. In this way artists as a professional group are also a product of modern society, a result of the mad rush of our times .

Through the Sami life-style, each moment of life becomes an artistic experience. Carving with a knife, colourful clothes with belt, cap and scarf, white moccasins on the snow, isn't it a dance, even if the steps may be unsteady from time to time? Isn't it beautiful when folk sit down in the snow, make a fire and gather round the flames?

So the Sami artist is a new product. Like Sami art. But cassettes and books have made their entry into Samiland, along with the car, the telephone, and above all radio and television. The last two appliances demand that Sami art exist: it is vital to the culture that it be able to absorb new and strange elements, and mould these into its own forms.

A successful culture battle can only be fought if we adopt the

---

* True in 1971, happily this is no longer entirely true.

same weapons as those the others already have, and at the same time take care to use them in our own way. (As a pacifist, I dissociate myself from the military terms. . . .)

Leisure

In the mountains leisure is no problem. All one's time is spent in making life livable.

But in the built-up areas it's a problem. There's electricity, there are houses. There are young people.

But there are no gathering places, no cinemas, no dances. This is true with few exceptions.

Not even the television works properly, and the radio's not much better.

There are now bars where you can buy low-alcohol beer. In one corner of each bar there's a jukebox. That instrument of sorcery which must be propitiated with mark, howling strange rhythms into the ears of the Sami boys.

They sit there, shifting restlessly on their seats.

Same old affairs. Same old faces.

Where there are only a few people, it's a good opportunity to keep an eye on each of them.

So your steps are well watched. Your words are picked up by many kinds of ears, and are interpreted in many ways.

If you stand when others sit, you already have a label attached to you. Strange type.

Don't think you're better than us.

Don't smile at us.

Do you think we don't know anything about you?

Not all the youngsters go to school. Not all those who don't go to school are reindeer herders.

When the school pupils have holidays and the herders chance to come down to the villages, time goes quickly. The latest news has to be told. When the reindeer herders come, the villages liven up. Money changes hands. Things happen. Then when the quiet times come, they have all this to remember.

Admittedly there's a church in most villages. It's very visible. But it's a bit bleak for the youngsters there too. Then there's the school. But the teachers are so venerable. Important people. They can't join the young people in any teamwork.

The newspaper comes. *Helsingin Sanomat* is a day old when it gets here.

Occasionally there are films.

There are also dances from time to time, oftener now than before.

But it feels strange to go there too, when there are only a few couples all told. You feel lost.

Girls.

Yes, there are some.

But girls vanish so easily from the landscape. They travel here and there.

Some become domestic helps. Some housewives. Waitresses.

A few stay, but they attach themselves to somebody pretty soon.

All in all, one ends up pretty girl-less.

The reindeer herders are worst off. At the same time, they have their own advantages. The tourist girls in particular are interested in the reindeer fellows.

Romance blossoms in Samiland, you see.

We've grown out of our infant shoes in a way.

By that I mean that reindeer hair isn't necessarily looked down upon any longer.

But when the social gap is small, stress must be laid on refinement. When a girl has been two months in service in Helsinki, she can't speak Finnish any longer, let alone Sami.*

Fortunately, the situation is improving.

Reindeer hair has even become fashionable.

* Social snobs regard Swedish as more 'refined' than Finnish.

Healing, Then and Now

There are many stories about folk medicine in Sami narrative
tradition. A mixture of fact and superstition, probably. Most of
the material has not been investigated.

That applies both to the use of graveyard soil,* and inducing
bleeding to stop.

Many substances in the human body have been recognized as
being capable of poisoning, and even of causing death. So the
tales of graveyard soil may be true enough. I've never partaken of
graveyard soil, so I don't know. But I've seen something of that
nature. I've also seen bleeding being stopped according to all the
rules of the art.

I've seen other things from time to time.

Like for example the doctors who've been sent up here to the
north.

I haven't actually seen much of these people, because they have
a special talent for disappearing.

If you want an appointment, you have to sit and wait half the
day, and then it depends on whether the doctor is in a fit state to
receive patients.

If you're lucky enough to get to talk to the doctor, he just eyes
you up and down and states: 'You are perfectly healthy. Just go
up into the mountains and keep skiing.' Even if the patient was
already in bad shape, he'd hardly faint with joy at such a pro-
nouncement.

*In the year 1866, the Russian government re-established the
right of the Samis to the fishing in the Petsamo district, but*

---

* A drink made from graveyard soil is reputed to have special
powers.

63

They sent us their school medicine from the 'enlightened world'. We have our folk medicine from days of old, which the arrogant call quackery.

despite this they allowed immigrants to settle there without consulting the tent-dwellers. (T.I. Itkonen.)

The stock exchange lies in the middle of the market square, surrounded by about 40 market stalls. Various Sami dialects, Finnish, Norwegian, Swedish and Russian are spoken. The nomadic Samis are the most frequent guests there, and they are the ones the bourgeoisie of Tornio and the farmers of Sodankylä and Kemijärvi make most profit from. Business always begins with a drink. The Samis are always afraid to take the first tot, but the businessmen always buy a welcome round, and besides, they drink themselves. They generally take it upon themselves to look after the Samis' goods, and treat the Samis well as long as festivities last; and when they are over, they just fill up their glasses, and say accounts are even, without working out any balance sheet. (Jaakko Fellman)

Then travels through Samiland of a new type, based on more idealistic grounds, came into being. Læstadian preachers used to travel round the Sami villages in winter, sometimes in all three kingdoms, and they were given lodging during their sermonizing travels. Brothers in belief, and the 'awakened' gave the travelling preachers whole carcasses, cheeses, marrow bones, pelts for garments, and even draft reindeer. A preacher might at times have with him two 'extra loads' of goods which he unloaded at some storage place or other.

(T.I. Itkonen)

Christ

There are already accounts of the preaching of Christianity amongst the Samis from the time of Bishop Adelbert of Bremen (1045–72).

When it came to the ear of King Kristian IV of Denmark that there will still heathens in his kingdom, he gave orders, in 1609, that all Samis who could be proved to live in a state of paganism and would not convert willingly should be punished by death.

The Samis had to submit to baptism under a greater or lesser degree of pressure from early on. The Greek Orthodox Church got a foot in Petsamo when the church which Trifoni had built was enlarged into a monastery in the year 1550 (or 1556). At about the same time the Church got a foothold in the west too, when three brothers built a church two miles south of Kilpisjärvi, in Rounala.

The conversion of Samis often involved violence, for the priests hung on to their privileges, disciplined the people with all sorts of weapons, and introduced spirits into Samiland. The best known is probably 'Tuderus, Christ's clergyman, hated here in Samiland'. He banished the shaman drums. Sometimes he took his wife with him, and had the Samis give her rides and presents.

Even granting the Church the honour of introducing the art of reading, she still has to answer for many kinds of comportment which one wouldn't have imagined were in place in Christian circles. I'm thinking of the last steps the *dačču̯as* took in their policy of impoverishment. As if it wasn't enough that the Samis had been robbed of their material goods; no, to really finish the job, they had to carry out spiritual devastation as well.

Like other *dačču̯as*, these spiritual men also used violence and alcohol as weapons, and a good deal of psychological pressure into the bargain.

This form of terror isn't merely a matter of history, it exists to this very day.

In times gone by people were condemned to death for *yoiking*, and *yoik* is still not accepted amongst the faithful. Just as a lot of other things are forbidden. Television. Fun.

I don't know whether the preachers themselves realize what sort of activity they are engaged in. They used to go from village to village, holding meetings. The sermons lasted for hours, and didn't end until just about the whole gathering was weeping and screaming in wild hysteria.

Since the preachers were spreading God's word, people often gave them the last joint of smoked meat, because it was important that these spiritual men got something. Of course it wasn't payment, just a little gift; God obviously took care of his own. The preachers might easily return from their sermonizing journeys with a great load of meat.

I cannot call the activities which the faithful engaged in anything but terrorism.

Christ was one of the colonialists' most vital weapons — so was the bottle.

Neither can I help seeing pagan characteristics in it.

But may they be forgiven for it. It is not for mankind to condemn.

So how can the preachers condemn?

They sow fear in the human heart, and create Hell here on Earth.

In my opinion it is truly fiendish to organize terror in the name of God, so that people who already have one foot in the grave weep and gnash their teeth. But in heaven we get our reward.

Even if religion is not a matter of reason, I can't help being astonished that God can be behind this sort of activity. It's especially bad when you know that folk are particularly susceptible to anxiety because of their hard living conditions.

In these parts, with the hard climate and the long dark-period, it should be forbidden to conjure up visions of hell.

The Law

In these things I place my trust.

The law came into being before me, and will remain after my days are numbered.

Amen.

The legal position of Samis is insecure.

The situation of the East Samis is becoming common knowledge; it's been made a public affair. The nomadic Samis of Enontekiö are at the back of beyond: out of sight and out of mind. There are about 400 of them altogether, and a good half of them live off reindeer husbandry. In winter they migrate a couple of hundred kilometres south with the animals. These days they move largely with the help of motorized vehicles. Only a few

The sword pointed at the Sami people can take many forms . . .

own land. The explanation for this lies partly in these migrations, partly in the Sami view that ground cannot be owned. The situation is completely crazy.

The Samis' right to the land was once legally laid down. In 1584, for example, the Samis of Enontekiö were granted the right of control over, and of making use of the resources of, an area which corresponds almost to the whole district. Comparable rights were granted to the Samis in other districts too.

Morally, these areas belong to the Samis to this day. It wasn't until 1886 that a forestry law was introduced, which stated that the area outside populated districts belonged to the State should no one be able to demonstrate grounds for ownership.

A bare hundred years later (1969) the reindeer husbandry act was put into practice. It gave the nomadic Samis the right to buy their ground back, or rather the right to buy a little bit of the ground back. The reindeer owner can humbly send in a written application, which may be approved if the public authorities decide he needs the ground. That's to stress that it's the State which owns the land.

Sweden has granted her Samis a clearly defined area. It stretches down as far south as Jämtland, and within this area no non-Sami may lease a piece of land without permission from the local council, and then only on the condition that the building does not obstruct reindeer husbandry and subsidiary sources of income which are tied up with it. If deleterious effects can be demonstrated, the Samis have a right to compensation. The proceeds go undiminished to the Samis; but with us in Finland, not a penny goes to benefit the Samis. Norway is also beginning to accept that the Samis have a right to the land they have lived on and put to use for generations. Our neighbour lands also seem to be starting in other ways to recognize that Samis exist. At the school in Kautokeino, pupils can choose between Sami and Norwegian as language of instruction during their first school years. Those whose first language is Sami, begin gradually with Norwegian after two years. Scientific investigations have produced evidence that pupils learn both their mother language and foreign languages best if they first get a solid grounding in their mother-tongue. At the secondary school in Karasjok one can take Sami right up to *Eksamen Artium.* [approximately equivalent to English 'A' Level]. In the Swedish region, Sami was given a place in the schools long ago, and in addition there are *sameskolor*, in which reindeer husbandry is a subject.

Behind the laws of the dominant society there is another culture, and frequently another system of values. Besides that, the laws are usually written in a language which Samis haven't been able to read. When the laws came into being, they were just as remote as the places where the word of the law is written. But today distances are smaller, and the consequences of the text of the law are beginning to be perceptible to Samis. These laws are just as little justifiable as if the Samis should start writing laws in which they maintain that Oslo belongs to Samiland, and that Norwegians are to be taxable to Samiland — besides which, all legal proceedings should naturally take place in Sami.

Schooling

There's been progress since I learned the ABC, and what 'plough', 'harrow' and 'street' are. There's been a Sami ABC book published, in which both text and illustrations are relevant to our own times, and subjects which are familiar to Sami children are included.*

Siiri Magga-Miettunen's ABC was really welcome. Learning to read isn't a game for everybody, especially when one understands nothing at all of what one's trying to read. Even if Sami children nowadays speak Finnish after a fashion even before they start school, the language they meet in books is still strange to them. The contents are usually drawn from environments which are unknown in Samiland, and the books talk about things which many Samis never come into contact with in their lives. In addition to the technique of reading itself, the Sami children have to learn to inflect Finnish words correctly. When they come upon totally unknown concepts, it's hardly to be wondered at if some of them just sit and chew their nails.

The way our competitive society works, the first advantage is often decisive for the end results. If one starts behind the others as a child, it's easy for the gap to widen progressively as one goes forward through life. Now people find it easy to believe that this applies categorically, because they've had it impressed upon them so often. Thus many Samis humbly accept their place to be the lowest rung of the social ladder.

Even if this doesn't apply to everybody, the exceptions only go to prove the rule. Language is often an obstacle for Samis throughout their lives. Their native language is supplanted, and there are many who never get a proper grasp of Finnish either. I

* A number of other similar books have also come out since 1971.

Map 5: Schools in the Sami Part of Finland

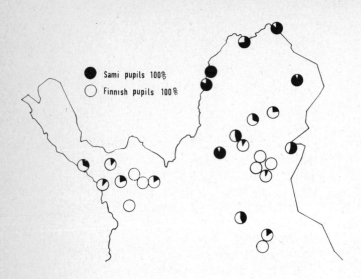

- ● Sami pupils 100%
- ○ Finnish pupils 100%

doubt whether it can be in Finland's interest to put the Samis in a position where they find themselves without a language. Instruction in Sami is relegated to the individual teacher, and to the local school council, and the whole job is performed purely on a hobby basis.

In the Finnish region at least, the Sami language has come up against an extremely negative attitude at all times. The parish priest of Kemi from 1757–72, Pastor H. Zimmerman, forbade people to speak Sami, even in their homes. Once, in Sompio, a husband said something to the children in Sami, while the pastor was listening. Zimmerman got angry, grabbed a stick, and threatened to strike the man if he used 'the Devil's language' once more. The man was afraid, and flew around the room shouting: 'Good friends, come and hear, the pastor is preaching.'

A tale?

Tuomi Irkonen, pastor and author of a Sami ABC, relates that the fate of the ABC was to remain lying in the school inspector's

loft. He himself found the ABC in the dark loft. These books should have been in use in schools in Enontekiö, but they never got farther than the school inspector. I was at school myself at that time, and I can confirm that no such ABC books were to be found at that school. Mind you, the teacher didn't speak Sami either, so maybe it came to the same thing in the end.

Somebody from Anar (Inari) once told me that the headmaster refused to write on his testimonial that his mother-tongue was Sami. When the person concerned insisted nevertheless, the headmaster wrote: 'In the family circle Sami is spoken from time to time.' This happened in Anno Domini 1970.

Today there are teachers whose native language is Sami, but by no means all of them get positions in schools where there's really a use for them. Knowledge of Sami is not considered a qualification when the school council considers applicants, and teachers with another background may easily be appointed instead of the Sami speakers.

The school inspectors can't be blamed for everything. Often

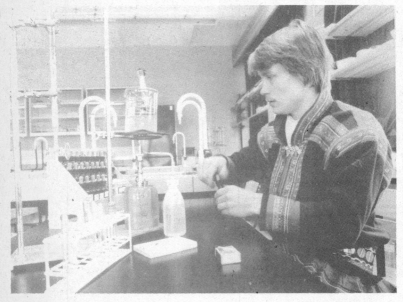

The instruction offered is ill-suited to our needs . . . few youngsters find any use for it.

the Sami parents themselves don't want their children to learn Sami. This is the result of the language policy which has been pursued. These parents have themselves had the experience of falling short in competition with the majority, so they want to spare their children the same thing. Many believe that the best thing to do is to suppress Sami in favour of Finnish. The parents' reaction is understandable, but one must put the question of whether society has the right to lead people into such a dilemma.

By the end of the 1960s it was possible to start noticing an improvement in the position of Sami. It has now become a teaching subject in many schools, and there are more Sami teachers. All the same, instruction in reindeer husbandry and in other special subjects could be arranged by appointing peripatetic teachers. In autumn 1970 the State appointed a committee to investigate the school question in Sami districts.

In addition to deficient education, Sami children have to go into the strait-jacket of boarding school life. The staff always come from outside and only speak Finnish. Clothing and conduct are not what the children are used to from home. Boarding school life is so unlike the home environment that it's not surprising if the adjustment process leaves its mark, at worst in the form of psychological disorders. From the point of view of the Finnecizing ideology, boarding schools are an effective means in the struggle against everything Sami. In fact these institutions can even promote a hostile attitude to Sami language and culture.

Great distances and scattered settlements can of course be used as an argument for not extending the vocational schools in Samiland. It gets too expensive. It's also true that a certain amount of courage is required to move away in order to get vocational training, not least for those who have only bad school experiences behind them. All the same, the Christian college of further education at Anar has had every place filled by pupils each year. This shows that despite everything, people do have initiative. If the school had some vocationally oriented courses the number of pupils would probably increase. There can't be any doubt that there's room here for vocational schools.*

* In 1979 a technical college was established at Anar ('Inari' in Finnish). It's purpose is first and foremost to cater for livelihoods in Sami areas, and Sami handcrafts.

It is also made evident by the fact that in many new occupations there's a marked scarcity of trained workers. Society can hardly gain by this.

People's self-confidence and courage to push forward will also probably increase along with their training and capabilities.

Samis still call each other by nicknames, even though they all have both first name and surname today. In the 1700s the clergymen often gave Samis surnames. In the church registers the following family names are thus to be found: Blind, Master, Hairypelt, Cook, Superfluous, Guenon, Blackhead, Lame, Firehead, Piss, Whitehead, Hammer.

And later appeared names like Parentless, Bad, Big, Black, Old, Skewhead, Naked Long, Unfortunate, Gorgeous, Undersized.

They were often caricatured quite openly: Thicklip, Inari's Giant, Proud Niila, Gorgeous Anna, Loafer, Flatfoot, Broadforehead, Fishhawk.

Samis still call each other by nicknames: Big Jovnna, Lazy Jovnna, Dark Jovnna, Little Pierra. The parents' names serve most commonly as nicknames, often being counted back through many generations: Oula-Juhan-Mahtte-Klemetti.

Mother-Tongue

Nobody knows for sure how language came into being. Many guesses have been made, for example that language arose by accident, as a reflex to facts and sounds which were perceived. Some believe that the oldest words in the language are those which resemble natural noises, so-called onomatopeia.

In order for a language to have a function, it must follow an agreed system of signals. Morse is one such system, and the Scouts have their own way of signalling. In well-known detective books they use code systems to keep information secret. In a narrow sense, language and speech are the same. Languages can be divided into groups according to their structure. According to such a division, Sami is a Finno-Ugrian language.

It has been calculated that there are over 3,000 languages in the world. The number is a matter of guesswork, because the border-line between language and dialect is often purely theoretical. Estimating roughly, 25% of the world's population have Chinese as their native language, 11% English, and 8.3% Russian. According to this calculation, every fourth person in the world speaks Chinese. English, which is considered to be a world language, is more strongly represented if you take into consideration the fact that it is very common as a first foreign language. This is true to a steadily increasing degree, and the new system of compulsory education in Finland places more and more emphasis on instruction in English.

In Zaire, there are reckoned to be about 500 languages, in the Sudan 120, and in Indonesia 250.

Of course there's nothing to stop you believing that language came into being in the Tower of Babel, if you want to.

But I shall allow myself to assume that sounds gradually developed into language. In the beginning the world was 'barren and empty', but Man settled ever in new places, and took over the world. Language developed and altered constantly, forms were lost and new forms came into being. These changes also occur within small language groups, and if the group gets split up it's not long before new language variations arise. If the radio had existed from earliest times, the number of languages in the world would no doubt have been quite different.

Dissimilar landscapes and ways of living create different concepts. Occupational groups develop their own language nuances, and it's a well-known fact that the language spoken by the experts is difficult for outsiders to understand. If you turn to reindeer husbandry, you will find a rich assortment of words and expressions which have arisen from the countryside, equipment and processes related to the work involved. So it's not to be wondered at that tourists have trouble getting around in the multitude of Sami place names. The world is full of language barriers which a large number of people never manage to surmount. Even those who learn foreign languages know only a few, and learning them usually takes a long time. Spreading of information is often hindered by language barriers, and when scientific innovations finally come to Finland, they're mishandled owing to many different interpretations. And, of course, knowledge is available only to a few privileged people, as a result of the language problem amongst other things.

Learning a new language can be like learning to see something from a new angle. Language researchers speak of monolingual simplicity, and mean that monolingual people tend to imagine that speaking another language is merely a matter of using different words. Familiarizing oneself with another language can also involve learning a new way of thinking. We don't usually notice another form of monolingual simplicity, which is that the same word can have different meanings within the same language. Many disagreements arise as a result of our use of the same words, but placing different significance in them.

Even the word 'mother', which is one of the first words that most people learn, may have varying content. For some it means warmth and security, for others tears and blows, whilst for others the word is an indefinite concept because they can't remember what mother was like. The word 'spring' makes some people think of a part of a watch or machine, and others of a place where animals drink. 'Street' is sheer torture for some, whilst others spend their time there quite happily; for pedestrians, the street

Our Sami language belongs to the Finno-Ugrian language group, it is a most vital part of the cultural heritage bequeathed by our forefathers.

can be a place where roadhogs let themselves go, and for motorists a narrow lane where the neighbours roost and pedestrians mill around. For the pious the street can be a breeding ground for sinful pursuits, and for the modern, youth social worker it can be a challenge for their labours; whilst a young fellow will maybe have visions of beautiful legs.

But that's not all. A word can shift its significance through the passage of time for one and the same person. We notice that when we start re-reading a book we liked before, and begin to wonder why the book isn't so good any longer. Words are susceptible to wear and tear.

Language has a history and a tradition. Whether we like it or not, we're the slaves of language. It furnishes us with ready-made conceptions and opinions. The worst thing is that we believe they're of our own production.

We've learned from the comic books that when one American gives another a punch in the diaphragm it makes a sound like 'Pow!'; from a German fist comes a 'Wasch', and the Finns just say 'Pam!'

Language controls us in other ways too. As language develops, connotations tend to attach themselves to words. Words can get charged in different ways, and this can even cause a word to change its meaning. There are words which are old-fashioned, and there are words which are 'in'. Words direct our behaviour, words assign us our roles. As soon as we become aware of something in the form of words, we behave as the words expect us to. And the best of it is that we believe we're acting according to our own feelings and our own free will.

Sami belongs to the Finno-Ugrian group, but it's a matter of interpretation how far this definition is correct. Most Samis live in Norway and Sweden, and as a consequence many Germanic words have entered the language in the form of loan words. Besides loaned words, an increasing use of the articles can also be observed, word order is changing, and above all one notices the influence on intonation.

The Sami language has been in the unfortunate position of being purely of linguistic interest. I'm tempted to suggest that in order to be a professor of Sami, you have to invent a new spelling system, or at least throw together a new grammar.

Sweden and Norway have agreed on a common spelling system.

Of course, Finland has to have its own, and naturally insists that it's the best.

I won't evaluate the different orthographies, but I want to stress how unfortunate it is that there is no common orthography. There are now several text-books in the Norwegian-Swedish orthography, but there is only one ABC book with the Finnish. I think there's been about enough discussion of the Swedish versus the Finnish 'u'. 'Null' is 'null' (zero) in both places. It shouldn't be so difficult to agree on a common spelling system, since the written language is based on the same dialect, i.e. North Sami.

But maybe it's not desirable that the Sami language should become an instrument.*

Fatherland

I was born in Palojoensuu in Enontekiö commune, and was early subjected to the harsh realities of life, during the evacuation to the mountain regions on the Swedish side of the border. Mother is a Norwegian Sami, from Guovdageaidnu (Kautokeino). Father's family are to be found far in the south of Sweden, near the Arctic Circle. I live in the narrow strip of Finland which stretches north-westwards like an arm — at least on the odd occasion when I get around to stopping in one place.

When I started school I learned that I had no mother tongue.

Finland has two official languages [Finnish and Swedish] according to the Constitution, but neither of these is Sami.

* Since this was written, a common system for North Sami — spoken in north Norway and north Sweden, and Finland was agreed upon (in 1978), but, due to 'lack of funds' virtually no textbooks with the common system are available. Students still learn the old ones! A common system has also been agreed upon for South Sami and Lule Sami — both of which are spoken in Norway and Sweden.

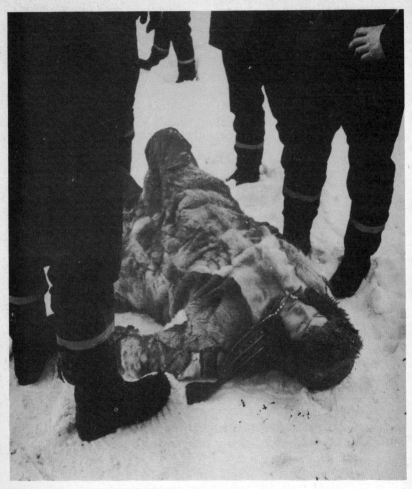

Our land is also trodden on by iron-clad heels.

When I'm at home in Beaddet (Pättikkä̈...
I don't have a fatherland either.

I live on a piece of ground which is re...
as so many others do who belong here.

Despite the fact that society has do...
aware of national boundaries, I feel r...
sitting with the Valkeapää family on th...
Luulaja Lake (in Sweden), discussing the harm...
the power plant being built here. Ought I to bear in ...
belong to different nationalities when I sit with my nieces ...
nephews in Guovdageaidnu (in Norway)?

So I find myself in the position of having neither mother-tongue nor fatherland.

If I were to define what, for argument's sake, I'll call my fatherland, my definition would to a very large extent follow lines on the landscape, and the gaps which are to be found between different kinds of livelihood. The mechanically drawn-up boundaries which are marked on the map are unnatural dividing lines for me. I will admit that I'm exceptional in having my family spread over three nation-states, but I think most Samis feel the same way. In recent times the pressure from the dominant society has been so strong that national boundaries have begun to exert an influence on communication between people.

Boundaries are a curse on humanity. Of course, they have their function, viewed with regard to law and order, but I think it's time people realized that the whole world concerns us. In my view, nationalism is a curse on the human race. Admittedly it happens that people fight, but we call that a fight, and not war. Nation-states force people into wars.

The Sami culture used to have the unique feature of common ownership of land. It was the strangers who introduced a new 'religion' in this respect. The idea of ownership used to be foreign. I don't think property and fatherland necessarily go together.

I don't have a fatherland.

I think I'm well off.

My mother-tongue is Sami, but at the ambulatory school I became aware that there are other languages too. When I started primary school as a six-year old, I learned that my mother-tongue was Finnish, and that my fatherland was Suomi — called Finland abroad — and that I belonged to the Evangelical Lutheran Church.

to read that in Lappland there is a people who are of
e race and speak a foreign language. Besides which they
l and dark. For practical reasons I let people go on
ing it. But it started already then: the Finns represented
selves as a courageous folk, as heroes, a people who with
d's help had beaten their enemies time after time. And many
ad sacrificed their blood for religious reasons at Narva, in
Leipzig, and the King had gathered the soldiers for prayers before
the battle, prayed to God to preserve his people, and then the
soldiers had joined in the hymn 'Our God is as steadfast as a
fortress', and then there was hardly a dry eye left . . .

Man is a social animal. It undoubtedly used to be a good thing
that people herded together. It laid the foundation for the
development of human beings into what they are today. But it
doesn't work any longer: the herd has got too large. There is no
doubt that we are in a dangerous situation: those qualities which
once aided Man, can now be turned against him.

It's disgusting to kill a bird by strangling it; but shooting it is
sport.

It would certainly also be distasteful to feel the last beats of
another human being's pulse between one's hands, but by
pressing a button one doesn't even have to see the results of
one's actions. But in that way a whole Hiroshima can go, and
maybe sometime the whole planet . . . a blood-bath such as that
at My Lai had the whole world in an uproar, but people have got
used to the idea of bombs. Agreements concerning the use of
tear-gas during the war have already been made, but it happens so
far away from us that we can't rely on the information which
reaches us. It's quite often a distortion of the truth. But then we
have the SALT negotiations of which we are so proud. Europe's
insurance conference. Helsinki, which is to be the congress city
of the future. Of course we can afford to treat ourselves to a little
afternoon nap. . . .

The whole world is coming into people's living rooms, the globe
is no longer incomprehensibly great, but a little planet, in a little
solar system, in the universe. All the same, it seems that most
people think along exactly the same lines as in bygone days. It
would be unrealistic to believe that Man in all his wisdom has
liberated himself from his animal instincts. It's true enough that
you don't achieve any goals worth mentioning through feelings

alone, but it's just as unwise to disregard the fact that it is precisely these feelings that are extremely decisive for the future of humanity.

A straight line of development goes directly from the masses to division into States, and today we've come so far that it's most relevant to speak of federal States. The heads of State stir up their subordinates in the craziest ways, and everywhere people are instinctively looking for a leader to whom they can subject themselves and obey.

I believe the development of the individual follows the same principle: I, the family, the immediate environment, the county, the State, and some people are perhaps aware that they belong to larger unions like the Eastern Block, NATO, the EEC, and so forth. After that the empty pages start. Nevertheless, many of the idols of the young (like McLuhan, Marcuse, Ho Chi Minh) are beginning to be common property internationally, and many of these point forwards towards global thinking. I think the young are becoming more and more aware that they belong to the planet Earth.

Based on this line of thinking, the concept of a fatherland becomes extended, and at the same time the ring is closed, so that we again stand face to face with the individual human being, which we realize is a core of thoughts and ideas. Each person is a link in the global chain. Individual fights individual, but the whole of humanity is composed of individuals.

Even if folk often aren't aware of it.

Yet.

Registered Organizations

There has been a gradual development of a series of organizations whose task is to deal with Sami affairs and promote their interests. They grow like pot plants. It can be difficult to carry out organizational work in sparsely populated areas, amongst folk who aren't very association-minded. In addition to the long journeys, there's a complex network of personal sympathies and antipathies to find one's way through. It looks as though the organizations rest on the shoulders of a few people, and if they should get tired it's pretty certain that the whole organization would soon fall asleep.

Samis now have organizations that operate across national boundaries . . .

The Sami organizations in Finland function in complete isolation from one another. All the same, they keep an eye on each other, and if the Nomadic Sami Party (NSP) should issue a statement criticizing misuse of the Sami costume, you can be pretty sure that the Sami Association will make a new statement in which they criticize the NSP for poorly thought out and unwise activities.

This sort of procedure is playing right into the hands of anyone aiming to work against Sami interests, 'because they don't even know what they want themselves'.

The voice of the Samis wouldn't be very audible if such bodies did not exist. But in reality they don't exist as long as some Samis are knocking down what others are building up. Perhaps it's important for certain people to push themselves forward. In that case it would be purely utopian to imagine a country-wide central organization for all Samis, for in such an organization many views would be represented, and above all there would be many important persons in addition to 'myself'.

In Norway and Sweden the central Sami organizations function and have achieved results.

The Finnish Samis ought also to form an organization which could speak on behalf of all Samis. And besides that, Nordic co-operation ought to be extended. Today there does exist one common organ for Sami affairs in all the Nordic lands, i.e. the Nordic Sami Council, but one would imagine that the moral right this Council has to speak on behalf of all Samis would be much greater if the Council were composed of representatives of the central organizations of the different countries. Also it might be an idea to include representatives from the county administrative boards, for example, as observers.

It would also have reinforcing value if the Nordic Sami Council could express itself on behalf of all Samis, independently of the country in which the affair in question actually arises.

Sami Parliament

Maybe it's relevant to talk a little about work in this field. There were spirited discussions about the position of the Samis. A couple of committees were appointed and given the task of investigating the Sami question. One of them concentrated on the school question, and was granted extra time for the work. This committee achieved some good results: in the Finnish area, it has been possible since autumn 1977 to teach through the medium of Sami. We've got Utsjoki College, where Sami language and culture are teaching subjects. Special thanks are due to the Sami teachers who had given up their leisure time and probably dug into their own pockets to write textbooks and other teaching material. Within the school administration of Lappi county, which constitutes Finnish Samiland, a position for a consultant in Sami language and literature has been set up. A Sami-speaker has been appointed to this position.

Despite this, the goal has not been achieved: instruction in Sami is not legally entrenched, and is still based on the charity principle. Teachers continue to work on textbooks on a voluntary basis. It is self-evident that the situation is unsatisfactory, as long as Finland's constitution is unaware that there are Sami speakers living in the country.

The other committee was given a more comprehensive task, viz. the whole Sami question. They submitted recommendations which include a proposal concerning Sami law. Even if this latter, seen from the Samis' side, is a compromise in the extreme, no further progress has been made with it. The proposal states that land and water in Samiland belong to the Samis, and that consequently they also have the right to decide how these resources should be employed. It still appears to be a difficult, if not impossible, matter to get this law passed. Nevertheless, it must be acknowledged that the work of the committee has had results. A trial election was held when the committee was still only halfway through its work. The results were approved, and with that the Sami Parliament was a reality. This happened in 1972, and at the same time resolutions were passed defining the home settlement areas of the Samis. In the resolutions it also states that it is the task of the Sami Parliament to protect the legal and cultural position of the Samis. In principle the work embraces all the questions which are vital to the Sami people. But there is still a weak side: the Parliament only has the right to express its views. It does not have the power to pass resolutions.

The Sami Parliament had new elections in 1975. It has 20 members, recruited from different parts of Finnish Samiland, but such that all areas are assured of a minimum of representation. The Sami Parliament officially represented the Finnish Samis at the Sami Conference of 1976. There the Samis ratified the resolutions of the World Council of Indigenous Peoples (WCIP), and by so doing joined the organization. So developments in the Finnish region culminated in an elected Sami Parliament, and the idea of a central organization has not been realized. In Sweden and in Norway the central organizations still function: Sami Ätnam (Samiland) and Svenska Samernas Riksforbund (the National

Association of Swedish Samis) in Sweden, and Norske Samers
Riksforbund (the National Association of Norwegian Samis) in
Norway.

An elected parliament has quite a different position from a
voluntary organization. Election is the foundation of democracy
all over the world. A parliament which is elected through casting
of votes must be comparable with any other parliamentary body,
and be placed on an equal footing with the corresponding organ
of the majority. Election by ballot implies a clarification of who
has the right to vote. In Finland, all those who are eligible are
registered, and electoral participation has been high in both
elections, about 80%. Those who are of Sami lineage have the
right to vote, but nevertheless an 'inherited' voting right cannot go
further back than to the grandparents. They must have recognized
themselves as Samis and had Sami as their mother-tongue. The
right to vote can also be granted on the basis of mode of life, and
on application.

In Finland, registration was a fairly simple matter, for Sami

*Parliamentary methods don't always work in our efforts to improve
our situation.*

settlement is restricted to relatively clearly defined areas. So there's no doubt about who has the right to vote. If one imagined something comparable in Norway or Sweden, a number of questions would arise. One of the largest groups of Samis, the sea-Samis, will not take part in Sami politics today, and many sea-Samis don't want to belong to the Sami people. Some don't even believe they do belong.

Even though it would be difficult to organize elections in Sweden and Norway, one should work towards a real Sami Parliament which would have local divisions in Finland, Sweden and Norway. Such a parliament would be in a much stronger position than the present Sami conference with regard to resolutions.

The organization of Sami politics is changing steadily, and one fine day maybe both Norway and Sweden will support a Sami election.

If a Sami Parliament is to have any real political influence, it must to some degree get the right to pass resolutions. Maybe we'll get that far sometime.

Nat Turner's Rebellion

The Many-sided Person

In speaking of the year usually one adds 'after Christ'. According to what the experts now believe, Jesus' year of birth was in reality not the year zero, but six or seven years 'before Christ'. It's lucky that there was an error in the date calculations. It would have been unfortunate if Buddhists had had to say that Buddha was born 563 years before Christ, and the Muslims to state that Muhammad's year of birth was 570 after Christ.

'Primitive man never looked out over the world and saw "mankind" as a group. (The names of races often mean quite simply "human beings.") The distinction between any closed group, and outside peoples, becomes in terms of religion the difference between the true believers and the heathen.

Our culture is different from other cultures, but not worth less. The slogan for this camp-in strike near the Alta construction works is 'The river shall live!'

Knowledge of the ways and customs of others, and awareness of how different these can be, is a step towards a more reasonable social order.

Even very primitive peoples are sometimes far more conscious of the role of cultural traits than we are, and for good reason. They have had intimate experience of different cultures.'

(Ruth Benedict.)*

A person with major aberrations may happen to be sick. Seldom because of the aberration. If he's sickly, the reason may often be pressure from the environment, which condemns everything that is different. So fear and frustration may gradually lead to

* Ruth Fulton Benedict (1887–1948). American professor of anthropology. (Trans. note.)

physical illness. The aberration may also be defined in this way: the person concerned has been born into the wrong cultural environment. In another place, he might well have been a respected member of society.

> The inherited customs of the whole world comprise a selection of different patterns of human behaviour which are so varied that all the variations will never be found in one and the same person, however unusual they may be.
>
> The life history of the individual is first and foremost an accommodation to the patterns and standards traditionally handed down in his community. From the moment of his birth, the customs into which he is born shape his experience and behaviour. By the time he can talk, he is the little creature of his culture, and by the time he is grown and able to take part in its activities, its habits are his habits, its beliefs his beliefs, its impossibilities his impossibilities.
>
> (Ruth Benedict.)

Different cultures function in different ways, but common to all is their readiness to set out guidance lines. Most people follow this rut, despite the fact that the rut can be extremely inhuman. It's really remarkable. What developed under Hitler's rule could scarcely have happened in any culture other than just that well-developed, materialistic culture in the West, where arrogance and obedience to one's elders took first place. Most people take over the attitudes and behavioural patterns which the environment lays down for them. The capacity to adapt to different cultural forms seems to be very great, and possibly arises from the fact that everything bound up with inheritance is very flexible. Most people pattern themselves on popular types in the environment, because in practice the interpretation of the environment is that those who behave like the majority represent what is healthy and of highest value.

> The pattern is not necessarily good for all. Best off is the person who has potentialities most nearly coinciding with the type of behaviour selected by their society. Nevertheless, 'normal' is clearly not an unambiguous concept. The abnormal are those who fall outside the traditional behavioural ideals in a cultural circle.
>
> In some societies homosexuality is highly respected.

Plato's *Republic* is of course the most convincing statement. He portrays homosexuality as a major means to the good life, and Plato's high ethical evaluation of this response was upheld in the customary behaviour of Greece at that period. The American Indians do not make Plato's high moral claims for homosexuality, but homosexuals are often regarded as exceptionally able.   (Ruth Benedict.)

Sexuality is the spice of life, they say, and many reflections about life revolve around this phenomenon. Thus, different cultures' views on sexuality give a good picture of them. In many parts of the Middle East, a woman is still regarded as a baby machine, whereas relationships between men are respected. On the other hand the Indians of New Mexico say: 'Everybody likes him, he's always having affairs with women.' or 'Nobody likes him much, he never has troubles over women.' Women's battle for equality is one of the most widespread upheavals in the Western world today. The expression 'marriage-deal' is well-known in Finland to this day. There are certainly many who buy their way into a 'forever yours'.

In some societies that permit polygamy, women are above all a labour force, but also a status symbol, like cars and TV. Of course there are also women who have several husbands, and there are cultures where women both propose marriage, and do the most important work, whilst the men sit at home over the pots and dig in the ashes, do the housework and sit and gossip with the other husbands. Jealousy is also a result of the rules and regulations of the environment, and jealousy is a very pervasive phenomenon within Western culture where the holiness of ownership prevails in all spheres.

Ceremonies to mark the attainment of puberty persist in many cultures. The marking of this milestone need not necessarily be a celebration of sexual maturation, but rather of transition into the world of adults. In central North America, warfare is a task for all adult men. In Australia the transition to manhood is the same as admittance to the feasts which the men hold. Women are excluded from these, and if they should put in an appearance nevertheless, they are put to death. Puberty ceremonies are symbolic and very elaborate, and are an indication that one is liberating oneself from mother's apron strings, and that one is big enough to take the responsibilities which befall a grown man. Puberty ceremonies may be the same for girls and boys, but when they involve only girls, they are most often symbolic of the biological changes.

The puberty ceremony in Finland is called 'confirmation', and is perceived by most people as an indication that the person concerned is now old enough to start preparing themselves for marriage.

Warfare is a social phenomenon, which some cultures glorify, other condemn. For the Aztecs, warfare was a means of getting prisoners to sacrifice to their gods. As they saw it, the Spaniards broke the rules of the game, because they waged war in order to kill. The Aztecs were so shocked by this disgraceful conduct that Cortés was able to storm straight in, unchecked, into their capital city.

(Ruth Benedict.)

For the Christian Indians of California, and for the Inuits, war is quite unthinkable. And despite the stories of Lavrahaš and the Russian robbers, war is also unknown amongst the Samis, even if some of us have taken part in preparations for war. On the orders of the majority society.

Communism and capitalism are products of different cultures. For the Pueblo Indians of New Mexico, non-violence is an ideal. They don't let situations which demand the use of force arise. They don't venerate wealth. On the contrary, their religion is based on the principle that nobody shall gather great wealth for himself. Thus a poor man may be elected to a high position in the priesthood if he has the necessary qualities. They don't develop situations of fear and terror, and they don't lay emphasis on sin and danger.

On the north-west coast of America, near Alaska, there were once Indians who were proud and powerful, and, under the circumstances, relatively wealthy. The culture was wiped out at the end of the last century. These tribes had great riches and the right of ownership was inviolable. There were two types of property: firstly ownership of hunting grounds and fishing waters which belonged to different families. Secondly, property in the form of songs and stories. The latter category was viewed as being the most valuable. They also had one kind of property which belonged to the family, but only one person at a time had the right of control over the treasure. The Samis used to have a similar attitude to property, with the difference that hunting grounds and fishing waters could never be under private ownership; rather, different families had the right to use these resources. Western culture has a different view of property. That is why the Samis have lost the right to use what they should have a natural claim to; they haven't taken care to learn the tricks which the majority society knows. There was a time when the Samis of Northern Scandinavia were in private ownership under the *birkarls*, who in this way acquired the right of ownership to extensive fishing waters and hunting lands in Samiland.

In the case of the Indian tribes mentioned earlier, the function of property leads a step further still away from the Western ideal. They didn't amass wealth in order to use it to acquire functional things. No, wealth had a function in competition with others: they presented each other with gifts, for example in the form of carpets, and if the receiver was not able to give equally valuable presents, he had lost, and the victor rose in honour and prestige. These Indians also said 'We don't fight with weapons. We wage war with property.' Somebody who had given away all his property had beaten his opponent just as fully as if he had felled him on the battlefield.

Does this sound strange?

Doesn't the credit system in Western culture work on exactly the same principle?

Back to the point of departure: deviations are not a mark of sickness in themselves.

> Amongst all races, there are particular individuals who easily enter a state of ecstasy. If this capacity is highly regarded, it becomes a routine matter to achieve a state of ecstasy, and a large proportion of the inhabitants will be able to attain this state. But if it's considered shameful, people will avoid such states, and those who have the greatest tendency in that direction will be considered abnormal. (Ruth Benedict.)

In Western culture, people are more afraid of deviation than of imitation. So an inconceivable amount of time and energy is spent in ensuring that nobody in the family is labelled a heretic.

School pupils often get a shock when they are made aware that they don't have the right colour socks. They have been brought up in a society where all forms of deviation are viewed as abnormal.

> We have to submit ourselves to the fact that moral norms also change within our own cultural environment. Tradition is just as neurotic as any psychiatric patient. This exaggerated fear of deviation from the accepted rules of behaviour is a totally neurotic feature. (Ruth Benedict.)

We have gradually begun to realize that there do not exist any primitive cultures from which Western culture has grown up, and is superior to. We are beginning to realize that there are different culture forms, which can't be placed according to rank, but on the contrary are parallel alternatives. There are no grounds for believing that any culture has found the one and only true solution to all problems.

> *Even if the Samis' right to the use of the resources in the area were supposed to be secure, dissension between Samis and colonists could not be avoided, because there was a collision of cultural interests. And quarrels didn't arise only over hunting and fishing, but also over pasture-land. Where the colonists found a suitable place, they settled down and stayed, and managed without difficulty to acquire right of ownership to the place, for the rights of the Samis carried little weight. Such magnanimity was shown, however, that in the instruction of 1760 to the superintendent of reindeer husbandry, they were asked to keep an eye open, 'So that the Samis weren't ousted from the reindeer pasture-land, from the bogs and the mountains which were useful only to Samis and useless to colonists.' If neighbourhood with Samis became too difficult for the colonists, it might happen that the Samis were driven away by somebody setting the forest on fire, thus destroying the pasture-land. (J. Fellman)*

> *In 1611, when the Danes attacked the Kola Peninsula and killed many Samis, the monastery took over the property they left, and, in addition, a quarter of the rights in Tuulomaa and their dwellings, even when the victims had descendants still living who were minors.*

In the years 1666 and 1668, the monks had falsified the documents concerning Tuulomaa, a fact which became quite clear later. (Itkonen)

It is depressing to read the ting books from this time. Samis often sat in the courtroom weeping and complaining over the injustice they had suffered at the hands of the colonists. In 1657 the farmers in Kemijärvi broke into the Samis' storehouses as well. (Itkonen.)

And the reindeer husbandry superintendents weren't quite honest either. In a document of 1607, Karl IX called them a pack of thieves who should 'dangle from the gallows'.
(Norrbotten 1922, p. 42.)

Aliens in an Impossible World

Humanity is on the march. The human race has awoken, and is not to be pacified. Thousands of steps are being tramped, kicked and run. A mass of humanity made conscious is on the advance, and neither by good, nor by ill, will it be stopped.

> Billions of people who are searching for peace cannot be taken captive. We have imprisoned ourselves in our narrow and petty bourgeois view of life. The task of humanity is to drag out by the roots the killer instinct which has so many ramifications and such an endless number of forms of aggression. It's useless to refer to God, just as it's useless to use violence against violence. (Henry Miller.)

Who knows, death may on occasion be an action which something may come out of. If only one knows how to do it at the right time and in the right place. Like Jesus. Or like the student in the street in Prague.

Nevertheless, this principle holds true: 'Nothing can create a new and better world but our own will to create one. People kill out of fear — and fear has a hydra's head. Once we begin the massacre, it never ends. Eternity wouldn't be long enough to wipe out the evil forces which plague us. Who sent the bad angel here? Each and every one of us can ask ourselves that. Examine your own heart. Neither God nor the Devil is responsible, nor are people like Hitler, Mussolini, Stalin. Certainly such illusory things as catholicism, capitalism, communism are.

'Who sent the devils into our hearts to torment us?'

(Henry Miller.)

There was a time when the white man needed labour. He used slaves. Most of the slaves were negroes. Today the voices of the blacks are making themselves heard. Today the voices of the blacks are toppling the American Dream. But the world is full of other voices too.

Colonialism reached its heyday in the 1800s. The culture of Africa's people was looked down upon; the fact that they had any culture was simply disregarded. At that time, scientific theories were advanced to the effect that primitive peoples, especially Africans, were not capable of creative work or theoretical studies, due to the mode of construction of the brain. They were simply sold as slaves, and it was commonly believed that the life of a slave was best for negroes.

> Something similar has happened in relation to the Lapps. Their culture has been denigrated, if not despised, by the majority society, if one excludes a few people who have specialized in and been ardent supporters of their case. The ruling powers have tried to integrate the Lapps into the Norwegian, Swedish and Finnish cultures. This integration has meant, in effect, trying with a clear conscience to wipe out the Lapp culture. (Erica Simon.) *

> If one examines this problem from the perspective of history of ideas, it's quite remarkable that this cultural repression took place in the 1800s, both in Samiland and in Africa, i.e. in the same century that romanticism and currents of nationalism held sway. At the time when Norway was fighting to free herself from Danish cultural hegemony, and trying to blow life into the old Norwegian language, they were forcing the Samis to forget their native language and their culture so they could be true Norwegians. (Erica Simon.)

*Erica Simon — French anthropologist. Lecturer at the Sami conference at Hætta, Finland, in 1968. (Trans. note.)

It's the easiest thing in the world to produce scientific evidence
that a people is not capable of creativity on the cultural front
once they have been induced into a condition where they no
longer have any self-respect and they've been placed in conditions
of slavery. Kwame Nkrumah, former President of Ghana, said
in 1963:

> We were brought up to be bad copies of Englishmen,
> caricatures to be sniggered at, because we wanted so much
> to be as refined as the British bourgeoisie, because we made
> mistakes with the language, and because our confusion over
> concepts led us involuntarily into difficulties. We're neither
> fish nor fowl. Africa's history was never told to us but at
> the same time we were constantly being reminded that
> we're worth nothing. What sort of future can we have?
> We were taught to look upon our own culture as barbaric
> and primitive. Our textbooks dealt with English history,
> English geography, the English way of life, English customs,
> the English way of thinking, English climate. Many of these
> books haven't been revised since 1895.

Nils-Aslak Valkeapää can witness to exactly the same sort of
thing in Samiland. Maybe with the difference that we didn't even
have our own textbooks; they were 'English books in English',
and the account can be dated 1971.

In his book *Turkmenistan* (stories from our own times), Jan
Myrdal relates a conversation he had with the wife of a French
diplomat. (She represented the Europeans who are capable of
cultural creativity):

> She described how, during the many years she spent in the
> East, she used to stand patiently [in] Eastern toilets, and end
> up pissing in her shoes. When I asked in surprise why she
> hadn't squatted (she wasn't wearing stockings), she answered:
> 'After all, I'm not a native!'

Culture manifested itself in that one 'pissed in one's shoes.'
The Dutch governor of Indonesia, Jonkheer de Jonge, used to
open with the following statement when he was interviewed by
journalists: 'We Dutch have ruled here for 300 years by the rod

and the whip. We'll be here for 300 more years. After that we can start talking together.' Early on, the British gave the impression that they had proceeded humanely against the Indians when they invaded the American continent. The Spanish and French often came into conflict with the various Indian tribes, but between the British and the Indians peace often prevailed. A more critical historical writer has jocularly hinted that this was pure chance:

> . . . *where the Englishmen settled, the hand of God made*
> *room by driving away or striking down the Indians, either*
> *by the aid of civil war, or by deadly epidemics . . .*

But this can hardly be the whole truth.

> *When the British met the Indians in North America, and the*
> *latter tried to defend their land, the British killed the Indians.*
> *In other places in America, and on the West Indian islands,*
> *and on the coast of South America, the Britons plundered in*
> *a fashion which Benjamin Franklin portrayed in this way in*
> *1785: 'A highway robber is a robber, whether he robs as a*
> *member of a band, or whether he robs alone.'* (Göran Palm.)

In the same way, attempts have been made to demonstrate convincingly that the Samis withdrew peacefully on the heels of the reindeer herds. The Sami legends which still live on in oral tradition have something else to say about the enemy and the battles with them. Historical investigations give proof of the same thing:

> There are stories of battles between Finns and Samis in
> Vesilahti and in Lauhanmaa near Kauhajoki. The Samis fled
> from Eräjärvi after they had had a 'hiding'. In Lapinlahti,
> in Keuru, they killed the last Samis who wouldn't convert
> to Christianity. At Luulahti [Bone Bay] in Keitele there
> was a man who shot an arrow at a Sami who was returning
> from fishing, and when the arrow pierced his head he said:
> 'Aha, would you believe I struck bone!' (Itkonen.)

> The mighty Spanish conquistador, Pizarro, invited the
> great Indian chieftain, Atahualpa, to his camp at Cajamarca.
> Atahualpa came, borne on his golden throne. In his retinue
> were thousands of Indians, and he was given a royal reception.

The hosts had prepared themselves the whole night preceding the visit by praying to God and sharpening their swords. In honour of the chieftain a splendid exhibition of Spanish riding was arranged, and thereafter the Spanish chaplain gave a speech to the effect that the Pope was unfaltering, and that the Spanish monarch had dominion over America. Then the Spaniards attacked the Indians, slaughtered most of Atahualpa's retinue, and took the chieftain prisoner. In captivity Atahualpa was treated royally, attended by the women of the harem, and he learned to play chess. In order to buy himself free, he sent for all the art treasures of gold and silver which were to be found in the Cajamarca society, not least gold ornaments, and when the consignments had been coming steadily for two months, the whole camp shone with splendour and riches. The great chieftain prepared to leave the camp, but first he had to witness Pizarro melting the irreplaceable art treasures of his kingdom into bars. Pizarro then accused Atahualpa of cheating, strangled him, and set out from camp to take over the rest of the kingdom of the Incas.

Christian civilization and primitive paganism confronted each other. (Göran Palm)

Nat Turner was a negro preacher. He was a slave.

He said: 'The moment you look a white in the eye, disagreeable things await you.' If you walk in the streets of Helsinki today wearing Sami costume and look 'whites' in the eye, it's pretty certain that unpleasantness will follow. Nat Turner lived in the 1800s.

At that time you could read:

> I owe Pastor Eppes 0.50 dollar.
> Use of a nigger for 5 hours.
> Asphenaz Groover, 12th January.

or:

> $ $ $
> E & B FOR RELIABLE BUSINESS
> CASH PAYMENT
> FOR GOOD NIGGERS
> $ $ $

Nat Turner, preacher. Negro. Organized a rebellion.

It was unbelievable.
But the rebellion was quashed. Nat Turner had no regrets.

> With one single exception, all those beheaded were buried
> according to the usual custom. The body of Nat Turner was
> turned over to doctors who flayed it, and made fat out of it.
> The father of Mr R.S. Barham owned a purse made out of
> his skin. The skeleton was in the possession of Dr Massenberg
> for many years, but later disappeared.

And today the white man is afraid.
Today the negroes say: 'The white man's heaven is the black
man's hell.' They also say: 'The whites came to Africa with the
Bible in their hands, when the blacks controlled the land. After a
while, the blacks had the Bible in their hands, and the whites had
the land.' The same sort of thing can be said of Samiland and the
Samis.
Today the white man is hearing black voices, and is afraid.
Today Göran Palm can be the white conscience:

> Since the Earth has become one entity, it's only reasonable
> that our view shouldn't be any different from the criticism
> which the Samis, the ousted Torpans of Gottland, the homo-
> sexuals of Humlegarde, the gypsies of Bandhagen, and the
> underpaid foreign workers have levelled. But we don't see
> it like that. Because we are victims of geography books and
> the nationalistic and egocentric point of view of the West,
> we see it differently. What if these billions of underdeveloped
> people were to come and say that our view of humanity, our
> religion, our historical writings, our conception of the world,
> our life-style, our manner of exploiting others is wrong?
> What if they were to say that in all these fields there's a big
> gap between our theory and our practice, and maybe on top
> of everything else that they had something else to offer,
> maybe something which could be a better alternative, which
> we would have reason to respect, something we ought to
> learn about, something which we ought to allow to influence
> us?

We are far from being equal as human beings.
Will we ever manage to get there?

23.11.69. 'Medal-winning mass-murderers. Women, children and old people shot.' Quote from the *New York Times*:

> American nightmare: information concerning deliberate
> and organized killing of hundreds of civilians, by American
> soldiers is shattering. These killings are so much in conflict
> with the USA's official policy that it's scarcely believable.
> Nevertheless evidence that frightening things are happening
> pours in daily.

Now we can read in Finnish: Song My is not the only case.

> When rich nations meet repressed ones today, be it for the
> first time for many centuries, or for the first time in history,
> people do not stand face to face. In order to stand face to
> face, they have to alter their positions. The repressed must
> raise themselves by at least their own height, in order to look
> into a face when they look straight ahead, and not to see a
> pedestal, books, or a fat stomach. The rich must step down
> from their pedestal so that they can see faces and not land-
> scapes, herds of cattle, (ore deposits, oil wells) or masses
> demonstrating. It's also desirable for them to see the face
> of the other, so that they see his eyes first; not the skin or
> the nose, but the gaze. (Göran Palm.)

Is Preserving a Culture Worth the Trouble?

Take care of. Conserve.
Nothing must change. But good gracious, this is what is genuine!
The opportunity to develop is barred by the magical words 'genuine' and 'preserve'.

Yet the Sami culture lives on, changes, and constantly takes on new forms. Still I am asked the following question: 'Is it worth-while to preserve the Sami culture?' But in the same breath, they state: 'Keeping it going is just a waste of money. It's dying gradually, if it isn't dead already.'
Brother, I answer you in the words of James Baldwin: 'Nothing can wipe you out but believing that you are what the white world

calls a "nigger". I'm telling you this because I love you. Never forget it.'

But what I fail to see as positive is the talk of 'preservation'. In a living society it's not wise to conserve a cultural form. If a culture dies out, it's proof that that cultural form has not succeeded in finding a viable form in the environment and at the time in question. Of course one can also kill a living culture through conservation if one goes in for it seriously. But pressed plants aren't particularly alive, and it's difficult to blow life into stuffed birds. It would be just as crazy to try and keep a dead culture going. Like throwing a dead butterfly up into the air and saying 'Fly!'

Whether a culture is viable or not is not dependent on how big it is, but rather on its capacity to adapt to new situations. In other words: the capacity to absorb new things, and find its own forms of expression, which are in phase with the times.

> Nothing is more certain than that cultures go under, come into critical situations, and are in a state of constant flux. A process of fermentation takes place, and internal and external forces constantly influence cultures. Negroes want recognition as human beings. A perfectly unambiguous sentence, with only six words. People who understand Kant, Hegel, Shakespeare, Marx, Freud and the Bible regard this sentence as incomprehensible. (James Baldwin.)

This question of culture conservation is of course touching, and reflects the fact that the questioner has sympathy and growing concern for the future of the little Sami minority. (Amen, it is finished.) At the same time, it's very illogical.

Why doesn't anybody inquire about development? Why doesn't anyone inquire about education? Isn't anybody looking ahead?

Or are the Samis to be a 'living page out of history'?

When I hear talk of conserving the culture, I see an investigator of folklore in my mind's eye, and interpret their activities quite literally: cataloguing a dead culture.

Studying cultural forms of the past can be just as informative as studying living ones. When I maintained just now that there was not much sense in conserving a culture, I mean there's little point in establishing a sort of living museum — zoo — where Man

is halted at a certain stage of development, just as one stops a
clock at a particular time.

Samis are expected to stand still at a certain stage of development, and everything new is marked sin or counterfeit.

Many Samis have this attitude themselves.

In principle it's worthwhile preserving and cataloguing cultural
forms, so that living cultures are traced and recorded for posterity.
The culture itself is not dependent on whether it's reached the top,
nor even on whether it's living; just as Mankind is not assessed
according to whether it's living or not, but is dependent on its
time, and what is highly valued at just that time. Is it important
to conserve cultural forms? The answer is yes, so long as it's a
question of a dying cultural form. But don't kill a living culture.

That can be called spiritual murder.

> The future of the Sami people will naturally depend on the
> decisions of the ruling powers concerning the Samis in
> economical, judicial, social and cultural matters. But the
> future depends just as much on ourselves, on how clearly we
> manage to put over what we ourselves feel to be valuable.
> In that way we can get a Sami opposite pole to the one now
> prevailing in Northern Scandinavia. Then we can get a con-
> versation going, a real dialogue between the Sami minority
> and the political powers. Political power is dependent on the
> attitude of the lower classes. If we can express our wishes and
> our view in such a way that as many as possible understand
> us, a public opinion will develop which those with political
> responsibility will have to take into consideration.
>
> (Israel Ruong.)*

Time passes, and what is genuine and original today may not
be tomorrow. I well understand that the culture conservationists
want to promote a development which preserves that which is
typical of the culture. But cultural conservation can be pretty
much a matter of chance in that sense as well. For example, if one
were to preserve the Sami national costume with the exact

* Israel Ruong (1903–   ) of Swedish Sami descent. Studied Sami
language and culture. Professor at Uppsala University.

decoration it has today, it would mean the same as setting a stop to development and putting the Sami culture to death: the costumes in the Guovdageaidnu-Enontekiö area are all different

Even if one makes a new Sami costume which is exactly like an old one, it's no more genuine as a result, and will be no proof of a living culture. In a way the Sami costume is a national costume, but in actuality it isn't. It's the Sami dress for special occasions, an expression of a living culture where each costume is different from the others, a characteristic mark of the person wearing it. In addition, the Sami costume indicates which kin the bearer belongs to, and in a wider sense where the person in question is from. It would be a pity if this development was frozen, not to mention the possibility of degeneration through an exaggerated impulse to decorate. Freezing fast implies a stiffening of the life force.

> Characteristic of minority groups is that they have their own culture. Co-existence with the majority group often results in their own culture disappearing, and they start to adopt foreign elements.
> — minority groups are welded together through a network of personal contacts;
> — the minority is also held together through a feeling of fellowship;
> — within the groups, an egocentric line of thinking develops. With the majority it often manifests itself in the form of negative attitudes.
> — the groups are kept separate through conditions of opposition. It's worth noting that the majority has a tendency to repress. (Edmund Dahlström.)*

The most conspicuous marks of our time are our mechanized culture and the standardization it implies. Ideas are to a large extent suppressed by fashions. They often seem to be all alike, wherever in the world they may come from. I find it repellent to think that everyone should be alike. Society is after all not

* Edmund Dahlström (1916–   ) Swedish professor of sociology. Author of articles on social analysis.

supposed to be there for its own sake; its task should rather be
to make life secure for every individual. The idea is not to standardize people. At times when I'm feeling really tired, I look
with envy at people who dress exactly like everybody else, talk
about exactly the same things as others, and above all live a life
which is so secure and so according to the rules that there's no
danger of dropping into one's own thoughts, and never the sligh-
test opportunity for making a mistake. It looks as though stress
is a result of the exaggerated comfort with which folk surround
themselves, and which in turn leads to ulcers and suicide.

Fortunately there are currents of thought today which are
opening the way for different trends. Pluralism.

> For minorities which are linked to particular areas of a
> country, and which in addition are few in number, like for
> example the Indians in America and the Samis in northern
> Europe, the development of the whole area is extremely
> important. The future of the Samis in Sweden is dependent
> on the solutions which are selected for the whole of Norr-
> land county. The depopulation romanticism which is charac-
> teristic of Swedish industry includes evaluations which there
> is every reason to regard with scepticism. It makes it imprac-
> ticable to solve the minority question of the Samis on a
> pluralistic basis.
>
> In order to define the position of certain minority groups,
> one has to be aware of the development which has already
> taken place. If the situation is such that the minority are the
> original inhabitants, but have been discriminated against and
> had to subordinate themselves to the system of government
> of the majority and organized collective repression, and have
> been promised improvement of their condition through
> laws and ordinances, then there is every reason for society
> to involve itself actively in the question. A fully satisfactory
> solution would be for the State to clear away the conditions
> which led the minority into a situation without rights.
>
> (Edmund Dahlström.)

If it's a question of numbers, Sami culture is probably at its
peak now. Nevertheless, one asks oneself: is it possible to develop
a small, unique, colourful culture in the shadow of a big, all-
consuming one?

At the same time, it seems astonishing that Sami culture lives despite everything, is perhaps even at its most vigorous, who knows — when we think that greater cultures have died out or been swallowed up by others which were even greater and more dominant.

We might ask whether Sami culture has any chance at all of succeeding, and whether we are right in proceeding with a battle for Sami culture.

> As everyone knows, the Third World — the developing countries — are ex-colonies. Samiland has also been a victim of colonialism, from way back in time when Samis and northern dwellers met in Northern Scandinavia.
>
> Due to natural causes, the first settlement in the area took place earlier than in other parts of the world, and for a long time the Samis were subjects of Norway, Sweden, Finland and Russia. But the political integration of these States has not prevented a continuation of the cultural repression which the Samis have been subject to.
>
> There is a significant similarity in this context between the Sami cultural struggle, and that in the Third World. An entirely new phase began after the Second World War. We are living in a time when colonialism is being broken down. All over the world new States are stepping forward, new nationalities and new peoples — often with an old cultural tradition. Throughout the centuries the West has been accustomed to considering its own culture the highest, and an example to the rest of the world — the African leaders see this characteristic as Western self-centredness in cultural questions. Now the Western countries have to learn to get along with other cultures, to familiarize themselves with the forms of expression of other peoples. This takes time.
>
> If colonization received support in its day from scientific theories which stamped people primitive and cultureless, then our day — to put it positively: the time when all the peoples of the Earth have suddenly become equal citizens of the world — must be supported by scientific theories.
>
> (Erica Simon.)

Fortunately, attitudes change. I'll probably live to see it confirmed that if a culture is suited to this time and environment, then it has proved at the same time that it is viable.

Culture concerns each individual who makes up the cultural community, both in their private capacity, and as members of the community. In this way the responsibility for development rests on every single individual.

All over the world, an increasing degree of acceptance of different cultures is noticeable. Cultural variation (pluralism) is the ideal at the moment. In the light of these trends, it wouldn't be surprising if the Sami culture developed into an important contribution. But only if it cares to, and if it is willing and able to absorb new elements, and let these emerge in its own special forms of expression.

That would be a start.

'Finally, I want to emphasize that the Samis' cultural battle — the Sami cultural renaissance — receives support from all parts of the world, and hence power, because it has, as Goethe's Faust says, the spirit of time on its side, *der Zeitgeist*.' (Erica Simon.)

The Bird has to be Killed to get it to Sit on Your Hand

The World's Indigenous Peoples

And so the ring is closed, as they say. Nat Turner was a negro. Once slaves were transported from Africa. Now the whole of Africa is in ferment. It's the conversation piece of the world. But the world doesn't talk so much about the descendants of the colonial powers who are afraid in Africa, and who are being transferred to the rigid dictatorships of South America. There, they are again in a position which gives them an opportunity to violate other people's rights. This time the Indians are the victims.

When I wrote down my youthful thoughts about ten years ago, I started with the similarity between the Arctic cultures. Today — not particularly old, but having forgotten some of my own indignation — I can demonstrate that this similarity is not limited to the Arctic area. Since I was quite young, I've dreamed of co-operation between all the indigenous peoples, not knowing that I myself would be involved in this work. Even if I could easily have taken an Indian as an example, instead of Nat Turner, at that time it was better to talk about negroes than Indians. So it was the history of Nat Turner which was related. The first meeting I had with the Arctic peoples was in Copenhagen. Those of us who were there can bear witness to a spirit which kindled enthusiasm and belief in the work. So I set out to keep it going, and we have kept it going.

The first world conference for indigenous peoples was held at Port Alberni in Canada, on an island near the border with the United States, from 27–31 October, 1975. I represented the Samis. It was unforgettable. Strenuous. For me at any rate it was an experience. A privilege. The fate of the indigenous peoples who were gathered there was so similar, that at the end of the conference the assembly stood up and passed a resolution to found the World Council of Indigenous Peoples (WCIP). The ninth Sami Conference at Inari in 1976 ratified the rules of the council, and thus associated itself officially with the World Council. In summer 1977, the second world conference of indigenous peoples was held in Samiland, in Kiruna.

There are countless indigenous peoples in the world. If any sort of reality was to be aimed at, one would have to have conditions for admission. The right of membership would be reserved for peoples who were the original inhabitants of their country, but who nevertheless didn't have the right to take part in governing the country.

People from various parts of the world came to the first conference in Canada. Amongst the participants there were representatives from North, South and Central America, Greenland, Australia and New Zealand, and Samis. All the same, there were many indigenous peoples who could have taken part despite the strict conditions for membership, but who were nevertheless unable to. Even though common interests, and their promotion, are factors which weld people together, it isn't easy to do a successful job, nor is it ever likely to be easy. After all, it is a case of an organization which spans the whole world. Even if living conditions, view of life and goals are common, there still remain so many circumstances which can obstruct work. If not actually bring work to a standstill, at least slow it down.

Maybe there's something symbolic in the fact that the indigenous peoples decided not to address each other as 'Sir', or 'Comrade', but rather to call each other 'brother', each in his own language, and similarly 'sister', as far as possible, or at least that's the idea.

The fact that many indigenous people don't have control of their own country, and thus aren't even in a position to decide whether they'll participate, or at least not the the extent that they can get public funds to cover the delegates' costs, doesn't make the work of the organization any easier. All the participants from South America travelled in secret to the first conference which was held at Port Alberni. Nevertheless, many of them were later imprisoned and tortured. The Nordic countries, with the exception of Sweden, have adopted a positive attitude to the organization (Sweden as well, after considerable vacillation.)

A world council which doesn't have the means to start its work immediately, and can't keep its members satisfactorily informed, doesn't seem very reliable. It was possible to get hold of money, but it was accompanied by the condition that, 'He who pays the piper calls the tune'.

Nor does it help the situation that the indigenous peoples live under such different conditions. In Latin America thousands of people disappear, and thousands are imprisoned. People are tortured and killed. Not so many years ago, hunting Indians was sport in Brazil. When you compare this with the situation in Canada and the Nordic lands, it's hardly surprising that there are varying opinions about methods of operation. Especially when you consider that the Indians of South America are by no means a minority, but on the contrary constitute up to 90% of the inhabitants of the respective countries. After so few years, it's not a good idea to make prophecies, but nevertheless it's natural to feel that the mode of procedure could be a very decisive factor. I wouldn't be in the least surprised if a thoroughly explosive rebellion took place in the whole of Latin America at any time. And if my brothers got hold of weapons, they would still have my sympathy.

One often runs on to reefs on the journey towards human rights. In this turbulent world there are many economic interests to defend in Latin America, and often no means are spared to hold on to them. But even if the organization's work has not really got properly started yet, it's still come so far that you can feel its pulse. The initial fervour is over, and everyday drudgery lies ahead. It's at this point that small organizations often collapse, not to mention world-wide associations with neither money nor labour forces. When it comes to working methods, distinct differences of opinion have already appeared. (Nobody knows what Big Brother with his human rights will think up.) Being moneyless means constant begging. And uncertainty. Being moneyless means that even if a general assembly can be arranged every other year, one sacrifices enormous sums on them. Especially huge when you think what sort of results can come of it.

General assemblies are held in the world, each one greater than the last, and they all outdo each other in formulating resolutions, each more splendid than the last, resolutions which no one gets as far as reading properly even once. There are already so many declarations in the world which ought also to safeguard the rights of the indigenous peoples: declarations of the United Nations which also include declarations of human rights. The conferences which the WCIP has held have by no means been of negligible value. Without direct contact, there can hardly be co-operation. In addition to the resolutions which the conference passes, and which are of value in themselves, one achieves something which is frequently overlooked: only through direct contact such as one experiences in gatherings such as this can the indigenous peoples get to know each other, and really feel that they are in the same boat. That they're not alone in the world.

The struggle for their rights which the peoples of the world are pursuing is of such a nature that it needs the support of world opinion. The world is to a certain extent engaged with the circumstances in Chile, albeit half-heartedly. But when you come down to it, Latin America is full of Chiles.

There can never be peace in the world as long as these peoples don't get the rights they have a claim to. For humanitarian reasons alone it is to be desired that the indigenous peoples, amongst others, should receive the support of world opinion concerning the claims they are entitled to.

Unless they receive these rights, there cannot be peace. But maybe the world doesn't want peace.

Together We Stand Stronger

We met for the first time at the meeting at Port Alberni, and the meeting was by no means an easy affair. Some of us had come secretly, with their lives as their contribution, and then there were one or two who had got there by mistake and took the whole thing as a tourist trip. The fact that Samis have a light skin, and some of us are quite blond, certainly had no positive associations for people who had learned to equate a white skin with colonialism and the terrible assaults on people which accompanied it. We heard about experiences of this nature, and I think the effect was pretty much of a shock for the Sami delegates who weren't well orientated about these conditions beforehand. Despite our skin-colour, we have our own conception of Nature, homecrafts and *yoik*. So we sat there on the last night, with the delegates from Bolivia, and even if the conversation was conducted in the language of the enemy, I think it went directly from heart to heart. It made it that much worse to learn later that some of the participants were imprisoned and some were tortured. I was in Canada again in autumn 1976, and then an Indian leader who had been at the former conference was in gaol. His children were at Port Alberni, and they knew nothing of their father. They doubted whether he was alive. I met him — Constantine Lima — at the conference in Kiruna in 1977. In the meantime I had learnt that he was alive and that he had been exiled to Canada, but all the same . . . in those eyes there was a flame, and his body told of torture, and I am convinced . . . I am convinced.

The objective of the World Council of Indigenous Peoples is easily understood when one knows that only indigenous peoples who haven't the right to take part in governing their own land have the right of membership. It's natural that improvement of legal conditions should be central. Economic independence is also important, and organizing education. The right to exist and the right to control one's own area of land, and the resources to be found there, are also matters on our agenda. Today there are many who would be happy if they were only acknowledged as having human worth. Though many indigenous societies are thousands of years old, it hasn't been enough to guarantee them so much as the right to govern their own areas. Not even in the highly-developed Nordic lands, where the Samis live a far more uncertain life than wolves, bears and eagles. There the Samis' pasture-land is proclaimed wasteland, Europe's last wilderness.

It is thus quite clear that the Samis have a right to membership in the World Council. At any rate it's reasonable to think that when the weak stand together, they may grow stronger.

During the course of 1977, I covered some pretty long distances in the Arctic area. At Easter I was in Kaladtliti in Greenland. In Ilullissati there were about 4,000 people. There were over 8,000 dogs. Next door there was a man who had a wife, 15 children, and 45 dogs. At night I heard the baying of the dogs. They howled loudly. We were also in Aasiaati, in Manintsoki and in Sisimiuti. We saw new houses and we saw motorcycles, and cars on the strips of highway, only a few kilometres long. We saw people dance the 'Whale Polka' and we sat in restaurants. Just as though we were at home somewhere. The beer-drinking also had something familiar about it, maybe even wilder.

I saw something in their eyes.

I also had the honour of being present at the first common gathering of the Inuits, the Inuits' Circumpolar. This took place at Barrow, in Alaska. And more and more those eyes tormented me. On our journey we came to the most northerly part of Canada, Eskimo Point. There we saw drunken mothers, who drank and spat blood. We also saw children get drunk. I believe I saw culture-shock in human eyes, only in a different phase, and I had to think of my own people, how they behave, and that the Samis are also experiencing the repercussions of culture shock, and of unconscious national suicide.

We travelled round amongst the Indians in Canada, from prairies to towns, and I was never a moment in doubt that we had exactly the same problem. Amongst the Blackfoot Indians we slept in the tent which they call a *tepee*, we listened to *yoik* and danced whilst the sandstorms raged. But it all felt so much like home.

Before the end of the year we reached the Soviet Union, and travelled in the area around the Ural Mountains, but I'm not going to go further into this part of the journey in this connection.

The other trips, however, were important in my opinion. The culture of indigenous peoples is essentially different from urbanized culture. *Yoik* is a form of music which is found amongst indigenous peoples all over. The *yoik* of the Indians of Venezuela is remarkably reminiscent of Sami *yoik*, in fact, even the language is very reminiscent of Sami. The function of *yoik*, its aim, was clearly originally exactly the same. The only difference is that here at home the Church has banished all the magic drums and removed the religious element in *yoik*, at least officially. With respect both to music and content, *yoik* has common features amongst all the indigenous peoples, with the exceptions of the tracts round the Gulf of Mexico, where Spanish influence has dominated. This explains the fact that *yoik* acted as a sort of common language, as a distinguishing feature of the meeting at Port Alberni.

Another common language was homecrafts. In a strange way homecrafts have so many similarities. Of course there are differences, that's self-evident, not least as a result of different access to raw materials. But use of colour, for example, was a distinguishing feature. On the Canadian tour we found that a girl from North Sweden had the same colours as the Starblanket Reserve, and that the Blackfoot Indians and I wore the same set of colours. I imagine they also know exactly which kin they belong to. In particular, bands and blankets were similar, both with respect to use of colour and technique. Not to mention the *komsa* in which babies were placed.

These travels of the indigenous peoples of Northern Scandinavia were intended to be a presentation of Sami culture, first and foremost music. Of course the travels were an experience for us. But I hope, and believe, that they also had something to say to those who saw and listened. What urbanized (standardized) culture has to offer today is so enormous that it's difficult for the various cultures to survive it. For that reason it means a lot to get cultural exchange between indigenous peoples going. It will also make the majority of people more aware of the different peoples and their cultures. I don't think it was at all strange that people didn't know very much about the Samis (when it comes down to it, they don't know much in the Nordic countries either). But I was really astonished over the feeling of kinship which developed between us, especially with the Indians of North America. I was convinced that cultural exchange has a strengthening effect, both for guests and hosts.

Global Perspective

Usually Nature functions rationally. Only Mankind seems to be developing into a mammoth in our time.

Culture-shock is the name of a condition where nothing makes sense; 'Yes' means 'No', and 'yesterday' means 'tomorrow'.

The indigenous peoples of the north have experienced culture-shock, one after another, most often without knowing it under that name. The culture which has labelled other cultures

We have natural alliances in other parts of the world, we should consolidate them — we can support them, they can support us. Then we are not just a few, but a big majority.

primitive, has itself approached a condition which can be called culture-shock — 'developed' might rather mean 'underdeveloped' — a condition which is approaching a world-wide catastrophe. When you look at it, you can't help comparing it with a sickness which spreads itself within the human body itself, i.e. cancer. Mankind itself is the cancerous tumour in the world. If you take the last 50,000 years of the history of Mankind, and divide it into units of 62 years, which approximates more or less to a human lifespan, you get 800 units. Of these 800 life-spans, Man has lived 650 as a cave-dweller. (Alvin Toffler.)

On a global scale, scientific and technical literature increases by more than 60 million pages a year.

> At this rate, the quantity of knowledge will be doubled twice during the period between the birth of a child, and the time when it finishes primary school. And when the same child turns 50, the quantity of knowledge will have grown to 32 times as great, and 97% of all available knowledge will have been registered during those fifty years. (Robert Hilliard.)

The population of the world has risen to over four billion. In 20 years it is calculated that it will have doubled. All good arable land has been put to use long ago. And the less-good land which remains is being put under the plough. But there's still not enough. The optimum number of inhabitants in the world is calculated to be 3.5 billion people. As a basis for the calculation, a ration of 65 gm protein per person per day is assumed, if agricultural production remains as it is at present, and that food resources were equally distributed. Even assuming that food was fairly divided, the optimum limit has been reached, and a large number of the people in the world get barely enough calories to keep themselves alive. A large number of the people in the world are undernourished, lacking protein especially, and even if they have enough to keep alive, it's not enough to allow for intellectual development of the individual. But the food in the world is not fairly divided. Three hundred million children are starving.

Far too many people die of malnutrition. At the same time one third of the world's population live in superfluity, and use up the greater part of the food in the world. And what's worse: a large portion of produce is thrown away, to maintain the price level. If the industrialized countries had not had a few small reminders of their own weak position, the corn bank would probably never have come under consideration.

The state of the world gives no special grounds for optimism, even if technology should manage to conjure up a miracle which would make it possible for all the people in the world to live reasonably well. If all the production in the world were really exploited, it's probable that everyone would have enough of both spiritual and material wealth. But this is utopian thinking, and the faith which Man (*Homo sapiens*) shows in it is a bad joke. This wise Man expends 350 billion dollars annually on war materials.

The effect Man has had on Nature is deadly. Especially those who have fulfilled the words of the Bible: 'Make all the fishes and all the animals your subjects', by being masters over Nature (and at the same time extend it to 'Go out and make all the races your subjects. . . .')

It has been calculated that the Americans, for example, have had 25 times as much effect on the countryside as the Indians, so if you compare these two peoples you would have to have at least five billion Indians before the amount of destruction was as great as that perpetrated by the Americans. It has been calculated that the world's population will double in 20 years. At the same time the ecological pressure will become six times as great.

Limited resources will not tolerate unlimited growth. Even less accelerating growth. It's worst of all in the case of resources which are not even self-renewing. Twenty more years at the same rate will be the end of many irreplaceable treasures of Nature. The same applies to many non-renewable resources, since the population will have doubled. In addition, by that time the Earth will be so polluted according to today's definition, that it will have to be labelled a danger to health. Where renewable natural resources are concerned, increased exploitation will only lead to ecological shock-effects, and to a total impoverishment. Intensive cultivation of the great fields in America has led to very adverse conditions: plant disease is spreading, the water table is sinking, etc. What will happen, then, when the rain forests are cleared? Maybe the result will be a new desert. Maybe the ecological system of the world will be altered. In general it can be said that the more varied nature is, the more stable and balanced it is. The diversity of varieties ought to be as great as possible. The industrialized way of thinking looks upon specialization as the ideal. That's how huge fields came into being. Between 1951 and 1966, food production rose by 34%.

But at the same time 14% more nitrogen was spread on the

fields, and 300% more insecticidal spray was used. At the same time it became clear that many insects had developed immunity to some types of spray. And it was calculated that there were about 250 types of harmful insect, and it would be necessary to increase the number of sprays to deal with them. It has also been observed that non-harmful insects are on the increase. They're becoming so numerous that they can be considered harmful. On the subject of sprays, it should also be mentioned that they don't only work on insects. A quarter of the spray used is transported out to sea, and inflicts damage there. Amongst others, DDT has turned out to be harmful to salmon fry. Nor does the ocean function as a grave for poisons. They come back, through the natural cycle, in the form of food for Man. The number of artificial chemicals has now reached over half a million, and for most of them there is no guarantee concerning harmful effects, and one can't prophecy what effect they will have in the future. To date they have managed to eradicate about 280 mammals, 350 types of bird, and 20,000 types of plant.

Mankind itself is dependent on ecology. The pollution which society is creating is another matter. Even if there's a way to limit the world's population, is there also a way to stop us dying in our own pollution?

If I were an optimist, I'd pick out some more examples of the state of the world. Something to dangle as bait.

But I'm not an optimist. Neither do I care to bring up more negative sides of the way things are developing. There are enough of them as it is, in fact so many that in this book you'll only find a small fraction of the available material. Since I don't want to be a doomsday prophet either, let it go at that.

But all the same, pay attention to one thing which is a part of human existence: on a trip by Finnair from Helsinki to New York, you can listen to all kinds of music. An orientation about traffic is also given. And you receive a warning: 'When you live in a hotel room, there is every reason to keep the door of the room locked at all times, and the safety chain should be on, as is usual in big cities'.

And perhaps even before you've reached the plane to New York, while you're hurrying to the Finnair terminal in the little *dorp* that is called Helsinki, it may happen that you've met stony faces on the paths, which have thrown dirty words at you for no reason. Overpopulation clearly leads to unhealthy states in people. The word 'stress' is applied to this state, but it's far too mild.

This population explosion must be stopped. If it doesn't happen voluntarily then it will be forced to stop. We have to realize that the population is dependent on how many people each area has the capacity to support.

The top politicians clearly take overpopulation seriously: the 350 million dollars which are expended annually on weapons, and the 'correct' distribution of foodstuffs, states it louder than words.

Let it be Said

Steadily increasing growth, and population, impoverishment of natural resources, pollution of the globe . . .

The water in the Tana is undrinkable. In the pools float dead salmon. Around Kirkenes miles of reindeer fencing are rotting to

The impenetrable fences of industrialism bring with them death and destruction.

bits, the cars in Kirkenes rust nearly twice as fast as those in Karasjok, in the mountains black rain falls. Because the planet is rotating, and temperature conditions affect wind directions, the polluted clouds from Central Europe precipitate precisely in Northern Scandinavia.

The atomic bomb tests at Novaja Semlja may affect Northern Scandinavia.

Thanks, I'm going to stop reeling off examples right now, thanks. We're getting off.

Genetic multiplicity is an insurance for food sources. It is a necessary condition for improving plant breeds, and for developing new hybrids which may be resistant to insect damage and diseases. Or against a difficult climate. All over the world varieties are being wiped out in favour of specialization. When an area of countryside has a completely mixed flora and fauna, it's called a wilderness. One aims at wiping out areas like this, right down to the last wilderness. For Nature, every one of these wildernesses is vital. They're often destroyed because their value is not generally known. Or understood. To the eye, such wildernesses are less productive than bulging cornfields. Or they're not close enough to the tourists, unless they have a motorway going right by, and a chain of hotels. And besides, people have a strange compulsion to develop and cultivate. At the same time, refuse dumps are created. And then you can say that wildernesses just aren't what people make them out to be. They are being used, but in an adjusted way. This also applies to Samiland, which is being marketed as the last wilderness in Europe.

For the well-being of Mankind, it is extremely important that the wildernesses and the marshes of the world be preserved. The Earth can't afford (pardon: probably can't afford) to fill with garbage such areas whose function we don't quite understand, and which may one day turn out to be irretrievably lost.

In order that hereditary qualities may retain their value, that they may fulfil their purpose, it is important that areas which have many species be preserved by all possible means. It is also important that areas of this countryside remain under natural environmental influence. There also exist peoples who have adapted to Nature so that they form a natural part of the environment, and live in harmony with Nature. Amongst these peoples are the Samis. (It's true that it might be a good thing today to add a qualification, and say that in this context only those Samis who follow the traditional way of life are meant.)

Folk who live in infertile areas without damaging the country-side, in many cases even supporting the natural cycle of Nature, may come to be extremely important in the near future, with the whole planet and the future of Mankind in mind. The Samis are amongst these peoples. Amongst my notes I find a short list, where 33 of the world's leading scientists, each representing his field and championing the future of the world, set forth the following, amongst other points, in the magazine *The Zoologist*:

1. Certain untouched rain-forests and tropical jungles and Arctic tundra areas ought to be protected, because we know so little of the influence these areas have. They are very susceptible to harm.

2. The inhabitants of these areas who live as hunters/collectors and hunters/farmers ought to have special rights to the land (or the land which they have traditionally used for their livelihoods) and they should be able to live without being subjected to any sort of subjugation.

3. Strict restrictions ought to be imposed on all those who are not inhabitants of the area (whilst the original inhabitants can move freely).

4. The area should remain under the government of the State under which it falls at the present time. These States are also responsible for guarding the borders.

5. A fund should be set up to enable the preservation of these areas. The fund should consist of money claimed from member States of the United Nations, relative to their gross national income.

So that's how the scientists view the future of this planet. And they add: we must avoid standardization just as much as categorical harmony in co-existence, and instead we must aim to create as many different environments as possible. There must be some reason for the Samis becoming members of the World Organization of Indigenous Peoples. Because it's not likely that the Samis would set out to support the other indigenous peoples of the world purely out of humanitarian grounds. No, the Samis have good reasons for becoming members of the organization. The Samis want their right to land and water to be accepted, and to have the right to live the way they themselves choose.

Let it be said.

People have admittedly been saying this, both subtly and bluntly, for centuries. Both we ourselves, and strangers. Here's a bit from a stranger:

> The fate of the Swedish Sami, compared to that of the
> American Indians, is in many ways even worse. The immi-
> grants to the New World stole, cheated and conquered quite
> openly. But as far back as the 1600s the Swedes promised
> the Samis the right to control their own land 'for all
> eternity', as it stands in the royal document. Despite this,
> the Swedes robbed the Samis of their land, and when iron
> ore was found in Samiland, they weren't paid any compen-
> sation. Later they were granted small sums of money, but
> these were distributed amongst all the inhabitants. The
> United States Government is now distributing shares in mines
> to the surviving Indians: the Swedes have yet to undertake
> such a venture to make amends. (Roland Huntford.)

This compensation remains to be settled in Norway and
Finland as well (that's a poor show in these oil times . . .).

> The Samis and the inhabitants of Tornedal, our classic,
> well-behaved minority groups. They've been repressed,
> ousted. When the way to education was pretty closed in
> practice, and the way over the old border was always open,
> at least for those who lived in the north-west, there were no
> obstacles in the way of a hard Swedicizing policy. At the
> same time it was easy enough to resort to moving south. A
> name-changing, and denial of one's own ethnic origin went
> hand in hand with moving. A group which has no power,
> which doesn't organize defence, which doesn't use violence
> in any form, that group can wait for justice until hell freezes
> over. Because it doesn't pay to be just to them. (Jan Myrdal.)

This view has gradually also begun to make itself felt amongst
the Samis. They want their rights to land and water to be
accepted. They've talked for centuries, pleaded and begged. Like
talking to a wall. Not surprising if such ideas are thrown into
yoik. Nevertheless, I think these are rare exceptions, and violence
is unknown to the Samis. In the Swedish paper *VI* Johan Galtung
says in an interview about terrorism in the world, and the reasons
which lie behind it:

> . . . there are about 1,000 situations in the world where it can

be imagined that ethnic groups have, or in the near future will get the opportunity to rebel against various central governing powers. The fight for freedom of the Samis is such a case. It's a question of how much Sweden, Denmark and Norway repress their minority groups. At the moment there's only one ethnic minority, and that is the Samis. I won't disregard the possibility that they may one day become aware that they are suppressed, and take up the struggle. Then I just hope that the Nordic governments are tolerant and understanding enough. Personally I believe in a republic of their own for the Samis of Northern Scandinavia. The Samis in Norway, Sweden and Finland piloting a State with its capital in North Sweden.

The Samis do not aim for their own State. That would be too unrealistic. When you know that great military bases have been placed in all the countries of Northern Scandinavia, and that in addition oil has been found, it's clear that a Sami State is a sheer utopia. On the other hand the Samis want a sort of autonomy, and that might well be the solution to the Sami problem. I really hope that the governing powers of the north will take up the case in time, and come to a solution of this nature. I am afraid that a terror mentality might arise in time, and that would be hell for all sides. Just remember that the Samis have never sold their land, nor given it away, nor have they lost it in battle. On the other hand, they have at all times received solemn promises that Samiland belonged to them for all eternity. Today the Samis demand that these eternal rights be honoured and that ought to be possible in countries which are the conscience of the world, and where the statutes safeguard right of ownership.

Samiland and the Sami culture are the property of the Samis.

A Bird in the Heart

I'm proud to have been born a Sami.

In my heart I know that without my people I wouldn't have been worth anything. A blue-throat twitters in the spring sun, at the life-giver, and a Sami future.

I look with special respect at the reindeer Samis, at this way of wandering in the mountains, the way they used to do before the snow-scooters came. But of course these are feelings which are gilded by memory, because my own childhood years were divided up by migrations.

Educated representatives of Western culture did their best to remind me constantly of how primitive the culture of my own people was. *Yoik* was not considered to be music, just a first attempt in that direction. Nevertheless, as it happened I became acquainted with sophisticated music during my schooldays: we sang the aria 'The King who was bothered by a flea . . .' In my heart the blue-throat twitters, but at times a cold wind blows there.

Today the world has come so close to catastrophe that we have every reason to blame 'advanced culture' for being the greatest danger in world history for 'underdevelopment'. Today it is really time to make a critical evaluation of what development really is. By being part of Nature, the Samis have adapted themselves for thousands of years to the conditions in their otherwise so infertile mountain regions. And what is best, these thousands of years have not scarred the countryside with the mark of Man. On the contrary, the Samis help Nature to maintain the multiplicity in the highlands by living there.

The Samis have developed a really sophisticated culture in relation to the countryside, but unfortunately, living feeling for Nature is dwindling, at the same time as machines and permanent dwellings make their entry. It is sad, because most of the Sami area belongs under what are called biologically vulnerable

To my great joy, I have discovered that those Sami youth who haven't been   ver-Swedecized, Finnicized or Norwegianized, have radically changed their course . . . all that is Sami they regard highly.

regions, and we have no general view of what consequences encroachments may have with regard to the equilibrium of the land. What we do know is that some peoples, like the Samis in their areas, have understood how to make use of the country-side without making harmful encroachments on it. One would expect that a responsible society would support and study such a way of life: it might, in the future, teach the world a philosophy of life which could be its salvation.

I have already been into the fact that the more varied the animal and plant life in an area, the greater the stability. Resistance to disease is greater, and the chances of surviving unexpected changes are also greater. One never knows how valuable an apparently worthless plant may be when unexpected situations arise.

Man is also part of Nature. The above is also valid with respect to Man. It's not a matter of chance that there are so many different peoples, so many different cultures in the world.

It would be boring if in all the world there was only one kind of flower, one single kind of bird.

But the culture of the industrialized world is trying to standardize people, their ways of thinking, and their opinions. The dominance of Western culture is based on the unprincipled use of courses of action which other cultures aren't familiar with, at least not in the same sense. Violence, that is to say. Exploitation. Killing. Today Western culture is living off others like a parasite, viewed in a global perspective. But gradually the peoples of the world are waking up, one after another, and the resources of the world will henceforth be distributed differently. What the West calls a 'depression' is only the beginning of a fairer distribution of resources.

But he who has might is right. And might consists of weapons, knowledge, means of transport, technology. By means of power one can plunder and control various resources. Oil wells. Mines. Economy. In Samiland as well.

Many reindeer Samis are bachelors. In this respect the situation is similar to that in many rural societies. The traditional means of living of the Samis have been discredited: the Sami girls have developed a taste for urban society, and are eager to go to Stockholm as waitresses, or to Oslo as domestic servants for the gentlemen, or to work in factories in Helsinki. And the reindeer Samis sit apathetically by their camp-fires, and don't have the heart to be really enthusiastic about their work. Because what's the point: no family, and conditions getting worse and worse with each new mine, or dam, or railway line. Such is the situation for precisely the age-group that I belong to myself.

But to my great joy, I have discovered that Sami youth — those who haven't been too greatly Swedecized, of Finnicized, or Norwegianized — have radically changed their course. Amongst the young, all that is Sami is highly regarded. It is evident that knowledge has been of use to the young.

Then there are others who tend to just stand and yawn. At the same time, the young have learned to use the same weapons which the majority society has used. I have a feeling that they wouldn't hesitate to employ a stronger language, as they have learnt to do from the majority. After hundreds of years of talk and promises, who knows . . . The Nordic lands are trying for a peaceful victory over the Samis, by forgetting promises, and not doing anything at all. Time and education will see to it that there are no Samis left in the future. The radio and TV especially draw the world in to the Samis in their nooks, not to mention the 'yeah yeah' which jangles from all the jukeboxes and supplants the 'la la'.

These highly-developed states practise their genocide by forgetting the promises of earlier times, and washing their hands. Maybe it's not done to speak of murder; what can you do about the fact that a primitive people becomes civilized and learns to live like other people?

But as this is being written, the sun is shining over Beaddet, spring is approaching, in my breast the blue-throat is twittering again, in the belief in sun and light and the spire of life.

A people which doesn't believe it is a people, is not a people.

This may come unexpectedly, but I feel a little wistful now that I take my leave of you. So I'll just wish you peace in your souls, and good health. Thanks for the company.

HUMAN RIGHTS TITLES FROM ZED PRESS

ASIA

PERMANENT PEOPLE'S TRIBUNAL
Philippines: Repression and Resistance
Pb

JULIE SOUTHWOOD AND PATRICK FLANAGAN
Indonesia: Law, Propaganda and Terror
Hb and Pb

MIDDLE EAST STUDIES

JAN METZGER, MARTIN ORTH AND CHRISTIAN STERZING
This Land is Our Land:
The West Bank Under Israeli Occupation
Hb and Pb

GERARD CHALIAND AND YVES TERNON
The Armenians: From Genocide to Terrorism
Hb and Pb

GENERAL

ALBERT SZYMANSKI
Human Rights: The USA and USSR Compared
Hb and Pb

DAVID STOLL
Fishers of Men or Founders of Empire?
The Wycliffe Bible Translators in Latin America
Hb and Pb

NILS-ASLAK VALKEAPAA
Greetings from Lappland:
The Sami — Europe's Forgotten People
Hb and Pb

INTERNATIONAL RELATIONS/IMPERIALISM TITLES FROM ZED PRESS

ALBERT SZYMANSKI
Is the Red Flag Flying?
The Political Economy of the Soviet Union Today
Hb and Pb

V.G. KIERNAN
America — The New Imperialism:
From White Settlement to World Hegemony
Hb and Pb

SATISK KUMAR
CIA and the Third World:
A Study in Crypto-Diplomacy
Hb

DAN NABUDERE
The Political Economy of Imperialism
Hb and Pb

YAN FITT ET AL
The World Economic Crisis:
U.S. Imperialism at Bay
Hb and Pb

CLYDE SANGER
Safe and Sound
Disarmament and Development in the Eighties
Pb

FREDERICK CLAIRMONTE AND JOHN CAVANAGH
The World in their Web:
The Dynamics of Textile Multinationals
(Preface by Samir Amin)
Hb and Pb

HENRICK SECHER MARCUSSEN AND JENS ERIK TORP
The Internationalization of Capital: Prospects for the Third World —
A Re-examination of Dependency Theory
Hb and Pb

MALCOLM CALDWELL
The Wealth of Some Nations
Hb and Pb

RACHEL HEATLEY
Poverty and Power:
The Case for a Political Approach to Development
Pb

RONALD GRAHAM
The Aluminium Industry and the Third World:
Multinational Corporations and Underdevelopment
Pb

PETTER NORE AND TERISA TURNER
Oil and Class Struggle
Hb and Pb

Zed press titles cover Africa, Asia, Latin America and the Middle East, as well as general issues affecting the Third World's relations with the rest of the world. Our Series embrace: Imperialism, Women, Political Economy, History, Labour, Voices of Struggle, Human Rights and other areas pertinent to the Third World.

You can order Zed titles direct from Zed Press, 57 Caledonian Road, London, N1 9DN, U.K.